Only In A
White World

Paul Barlin

PublishAmerica
Baltimore

First printing

ISBN: 1-59286-907-6
PUBLISHED BY PUBLISHAMERICA, LLLP
www.publishamerica.com
Baltimore

Printed in the United States of America

For Douglass, Leanne, Jo Anne and Michael

Thanks to Melinda Taintor, whose *Chicago Manual of Style* sharp eye found the elusive typos and suggested how to make sense of confusing sentences, and to Elizabeth Hardisty, whose dedication to the story helped to shape the early drafts.

Also by the author:
From Andrew, With Love
A Dancer On The Edge
The Yellow Line
All My Fathers, a novella

Chapter 1
Los Angeles, California, 1955

Senator Joseph McCarthy and his House UnAmerican Committee brought the cold war to a fiery climax in Los Angeles. They accused Hollywood of harboring Communists in the film industry who were poisoning the minds of millions of filmgoers. Frightened movie moguls, anxiety-ridden to prove they were not unAmerican, tore up the contract of any actor, writer or director named at McCarthy's hearings, no matter how talented. On the other side were those creative talents, who stood on their constitutional rights not to talk, and refused to buckle to the junior senator from Wisconsin.

To widen his cry, *AMERICA IS IN DANGER!,* McCarthy probed for anyone known to have talked to a might-be-a-Communist, so that he could immediately be fingered as 'siding with those who planned to overthrow the American government by force.' Organizations that asked for government child-care funds, unions seeking an increase in the minimum wage, any group of more than three that was critical of Republican President Eisenhower, were under suspicion as 'fellow-travelers' with the Communists. It was a time when the 'L' word, liberal, was cocooned within the *whispered only* category to never again recover its free voice.

It was ten years after the end of World War II. Negro families who had migrated from the South to war jobs in the North were the last to be hired in the makeover to civilian industry. They found themselves living their dream of being part of the American economy shunted into ghettoes of northern cities just as they had in the South. Many joined the great migration west to sunny Southern California where, for all the usual discriminatory reasons, most ended up in the inner city of Watts in Los Angeles.

A year earlier the Supreme Court had declared that the southern sham of 'separate, but equal, schools' for Negro children and White children was unconstitutional. It spurred the cry, "Integration!" from the truncated lives in the inner city ghettoes of all the cities in California.

But for many years 'integration' would remain just political speak. So far, it had not ferreted out the little known racist law, firmly implanted in the state's rules for adoption by the Conservative *John Birch Society,* that said that an inter-racial baby is a non-White, and can be given only to a Negro family.

That law slapped Jessica Keebler, director of the *Los Angeles County Bureau of Adoptions,* in the face every day. Negro families asking to adopt were as rare as rain in the Mojave desert. Inter-racial babies were piling up in foster homes. Teens, who couldn't wait for full integration, were practicing it sexually, and delivered more 'mixed' babies every week for Jessica to find homes for.

Despite the tensions that gripped the nation over McCarthy's red scare exploding in their midst, Jessica Keebler's focus remained on babies, those squirmy, needy bits of life that demanded her staff's instant and constant response. The all-White babies were no problem. They were matched up with a Caucasian couple, and after eight months, during which time the agency tested the baby to see that it was growing normally, the infant was turned over to the beaming parents. It was the inter-racial babies that twisted Jessica's nights into nightmares.

The swelling number of mixed babies held in foster homes threatened to explode the resources of the agency as well as Jessica's ability to maintain sane workloads for her caseworkers.

She walked up the steps of her agency fuming over yesterday's last minute phone call from Beth, the head maternity nurse at *County General.*

"I was hoping I wouldn't hear from you this month, Beth."

"Sorry, Jessica."

"How many."

"Eleven."

"Eleven! You can't be serious."

"It's spring. Teenagers like to cuddle in the winter."

"I don't have room, Beth. The *LA Times* slammed us last month for inadequate foster homes..."

"I know I'm passing the buck, Jessica honey, but I've got to make room for those coming in. I don't have options. They're lined up..."

"I don't either!"

Furious to have the inadequacies of California's social work system dumped onto her agency again, Jessica tripped on the last of the forty-two steps, stumbled and caught on to the bar of the heavy glass door to keep from falling.

Nancy at the switchboard looked up as Jessica stomped in. "Good morning, Jessica."

"As soon as my interns get in, tell them there'll be a meeting in my office before they go out on their rounds."

"Yes, Jessica." Nancy stared after Jessica striding down the hall.

When Jessica faced her five case workers in her office that morning, the 'mixed' babies backlogged in LA's foster homes numbered seventy-four. Jessica sat back and looked at her eager interns, facing her on folding chairs. Knowing the shock that she was about to impart to them, she thought, *Oh God, I don't want to do this to them.* Graduate students, itching for their first hands-on social work experience, they had enthusiastically signed on to supervise the care of infants in foster homes.

Jessica, to reaffirm her reason for calling them in, replayed her fitful, nightmarish sleep of the night before sparked by Beth's phone call; *A rushing rapids of ethnic babies knocked her down, tumbled over her, Asian eyes in light to dark skins, broad noses unexpectedly in whitish faces, a jumble of ethnic features and skin colors, giggling, crying, throwing up, reached out to her with their pudgy flailing arms.* She looked at her five interns, each already handling a caseload of fifteen, her promised cap. Jessica took a deep breath and exhaled. *And they want us to find homes for more mixed babies?* She wondered where to begin. *In any case,* she admonished herself, *don't give them a clue of how furious you are with the crisis dumped in your lap.*

Jessica took another deep breath and sat up. *I could've used the conference room, but it's too impersonal. I need to make them feel we're family, we're all sweating this one together. Can they handle it?* Jessica compared her equally eager, twenty-one-year-old self, doing fieldwork twenty-eight years ago. *Ah, youth. Each one'll either think she can handle it or kiss the agency goodbye.*

Worried as to whether these youngsters could relate to her, she compared her stocky, fleshy body to their young slimness. Jessica had lost an inch in height since then, down to five-three, and padded herself with ten pounds. Remembering brushing out her perky, graying-brown hair that morning and how it bounced back into attractive waves, Jessica smiled, not displeased with her mature appearance. *The shadows under my eyes are not horrendous, but the extra padding does put me in the category of mother as well as director of these snippets.* At forty-nine, Jessica had a fear of being thought of by this next generation as old-fuddy-duddy-stick-in-the-muddy, as she knew one supervisor was thought of by her young staff. Jessica felt reassured that her embroidered yellow blouse and printed blue skirt were as colorful as their youthful clothing choices.

Jessica was aware that her thoughts of being 'mother' to these youngsters was prompted by her miscarriage of a daughter in the second year of her marriage to Lenny. It made her afraid to try again, delaying her son Jonathon's birth until she was thirty.

Returning to the purpose of the meeting, Jessica reminded herself of the seventy-four inter-racial babies currently in foster homes that the five interns were supervising. These babies were secretly labeled among staff as 'unadoptable,' meaning *doomed*; they would be shunted through the system until they were eighteen, then put out to fend on their own.

And the babies keep coming, ran the cynical refrain in Jessica's head. *Teenagers drop them off at the state's door and go skipping on their way.* Looking across her desk to her left, Jessica saw the relaxed faces of Hulda, Grace and Emily chatting quietly, the three most experienced of the five, because they'd signed on in the spring and worked through the summer. Jessica sensed that they were comfortable with the agency's required paper work documenting conditions found during each baby visit. On Jessica's right were Janice Devoe and Alicia Varga, who started in mid-September. They'd been at the agency only three weeks and were still finding their way. Jessica scanned the five faces again. *They seem to be expecting no more than minor adjustments to their visiting routines.* She smiled to them, grimly, because she'd tell them they would have to supervise even more than fifteen infants. Jessica shook her head, hating to break her spoken promise to them. *That's what I told Janice and Alicia just three weeks ago when they signed on.* She sighed heavily, then pressed the button for the switchboard.

"Yes, Jessica."

"Hold my calls, Nancy."

"Right."

No calls? The relaxed trio stiffened, their faces curious. Grace, her straight black hair parted in the middle, turned to blonde Hulda on her right and whispered, "No calls, Hulda. What's up?"

Hulda shook her head but was silent.

Grace turned to brown-skinned Emily next, whose black, tight curls were cut close to follow the shape of her head.

Emily anticipated Grace's question. She shrugged, then shook her head.

"Ladies," Jessica began quietly, watching as their faces grew more curious, "I've called you in …because the agency's in crisis."

The features of the three older interns softened to cynical smiles, irritating Jessica. She noticed their metal folding chairs grouped, separating them from the other two. "Yes, I know," Jessica snapped at the trio, "the LA County Bureau of Adoptions is *always* in crisis, yet we're still here and functioning."

Her sharp tone eradicated the smiles. "But this time…" Jessica hesitated, to gain control of her upset. "Emily, what's your case-load?"

"Uh…fifteen, Jessica." Her brown face frowned. "No, sixteen. You asked me to take another one yesterday."

Jessica nodded. "Yes, I did. Can you handle five more?"

Emily's eyes widened, her mouth dropped open in dismay.

Jessica studied the others. *No smiles.* She couldn't resist the temptation to shock them further to make them understand how serious this mess was. "Janice and Alicia, since you've just started, you might want to reconsider your other career options."

Janice and Alicia looked confused. Jessica had welcomed them enthusiastically when she interviewed them and they made the decision to sign on for the two-year fieldwork stint with the agency.

Jessica had everyone's focus. Despite her own inner turbulence, she continued quietly. "We have seventy-four, inter-racial, unadoptable babies in foster homes, twenty-four of them in marginal homes. Two months ago, the *LA Times'* nasty feature article reminded us how marginal some of them are. Yet this morning," she paused, " I was informed by *County General* that we have to find homes for eleven more *'unadoptable'* babies by the end of this week...*more* questionable foster homes."

"It's *unfair*, Jessica!" Five-foot-eight Hulda was standing, towering over the others in the crowded office, one fist impulsively clenched, the placid pale of her face anger-red. Her intense blue eyes glistened.

"*Life* is unfair, Hulda," Jessica snapped. "*Too many babies is unfair.*" Jessica stopped, cautioned herself to calm down. She tried for humor. "We should picket all the pregnant teenagers, '*Unfair to social workers.'*"

Hulda remained standing.

Jessica waited.

Hulda's tensed hand relaxed. She plopped down with an exasperated, "Huh!"

"I'd understand, Hulda, if you thought of resigning."

"*That's* unfair, Jessica. You know I wouldn't."

"Sorry, Hulda," Jessica apologized, "you've been more than loyal." Jessica chewed her lips in regret for having insulted one so devoted as Hulda. She turned to the others. "To prepare us for the difficulties of the year ahead, *County General* let me know that *one-quarter* of the present babies in their nursery are of teen, unwed mothers." She paused to let it sink in.

"Are we getting them *all?*" Grace's voice was anguished. She leaned toward Jessica, her jaw slacked in defeat.

"No, Grace, luckily not, but even *one* more is one too many."

Grace nodded. "Yes." She sat back in her chair.

The others voiced, "Right, right on."

Jessica hoped her tone would make them feel she was on their side. In preamble, she raised and dropped her hands in a gesture of helplessness. "My cap for case loads is destroyed. The county supervisors *know* of our under funding for caseworkers, but in Sacramento, unfortunately, our budget allocation does not rate priority."

"What do they expect us to *do!*" Emily was up. Her blouse and skirt quivered on her trembling body. Palms extended in a gesture of helplessness, she expressed the pain of all of them.

Jessica smiled sadly at their innocence. Their first lesson in Political Economics for Social Workers. She knew the coming stabs of pain with each crisis would make them question whether to stay in their chosen field. She'd share with those who stuck it out, her deepest thoughts of the unconscious male cruelty toward social workers, as she had with her assistant, Roberta Walker. *It happens,* she would say, *because most social workers are women and the politicians, men.*

Jessica focused on Emily standing before her and silently reran Emily's desperate question. Jessica responded slowly and softly. "They expect us to keep the agency running."

"How? With what?"

Jessica turned her palms up, brought them together, one curved palm on top of the other to make the smallest cup possible. "With whatever assets we have. A budget increase must wait on state elections three years away."

Jessica decided that political babble was of no help. She laid it on the line for them. "So it comes down to us. We are the battle medics assigned to pick up the dispossessed, the wounded, under fire from friend as well as foe. This agency is where LA County's unwanted babies get taken care of...or not. Without us..." She gestured the unknown.

During the silence Jessica scanned the faces of her stalwarts, then lowered her voice even further. "What kind of job can I expect you to do under such circumstances?" Jessica leaned forward and whispered, "The best that you can." She sat back, grateful they were there to share her pain. *Alone, I'd lock my door and cry.* She asked quietly, "Still no thoughts of resigning?" and waited.

Their expressions mimed hurt, thought, anger. Then, in the lengthening silence, they seemed to relax. Small smiles softened their faces.

Grateful for their loyalty, Jessica smiled back. "Thank you, ladies, you *are* a treasure. I hope we never burden you so much that we drive you out of the agency... out of the field. You know how desperately you're needed."

"Carry on then," she continued quietly, wrapping it up. "Meet with your foster home inspectors. I've already alerted them that they have to choose eleven homes immediately from the applicant list. By the end of this month we'll need to find *twenty* foster homes...and think of possibly doubling the infants in some of them." Jessica spoke directly to the two newer interns then, "Janice and Alicia, you'll have to expect that your case loads will increase as well."

Janice and Alicia nodded solemnly.

Though relieved that she was able to spill the bad news without shattering the ranks, Jessica felt the need to calm remaining uncertainties. "Questions?"

In the silence she saw heads shake slightly. Her gratitude for their devotion welled up. She spoke more quickly to detour her tears of appreciation and relief. "Any time you want to talk, ladies, knock. Don't hesitate. And *thank you.*" Her added emphasis to her usual phrase that ended the meeting didn't seem enough for her. She went on. "For your courage, I'm proud of you."

The scraping of chairs as everyone stood, reminded Jessica that they'd heard, accepted, and would be on their way to do their jobs.

Instead of joining the others easing toward the door with their folded chairs, Emily Karelin moved toward the desk. "May I have a word, Jessica?"

"Sure."

The door closed behind the others. Jessica lifted the phone. "Line's open, Nancy."

Sitting at the side of Jessica's desk Emily leaned toward her supervisor in her usual earnestness, her eyes glistening, threatening tears.

Jessica flinched. *Another crisis?*

"We have to remove the 'Lee' baby from the Andersons."

"Remove?"

Emily nodded firmly. "Yes."

"Why? They did fairly well with the 'Jimmy' baby."

"'Jimmy' was White, and he was adopted soon after. They apparently can't relate to one who's Chinese and Negro."

It was a common problem with mixed babies in White homes. Jessica made a mental note to recheck the data sheet for would-be foster parents. It still failed to ferret out foster parent racial prejudice. "Where'll we put him?"

Emily exhaled forcibly before continuing. "He's in a terrible state of neglect. When I got there yesterday the Andersons were arguing. I heard them before I rang the bell. Mr. Anderson smelled of beer. The baby was crying in his crib. He hadn't been changed for hours. I cleaned, changed, and held him. He's pathetically thin. They can't be following the feeding schedule. And he...he...this poor child, this is the second home that's treated him badly. He's...he's so...so different." She compressed her full lips to keep from crying.

Jessica slipped forward on her chair to touch Emily's arm and hold it until Emily reined herself in. "Try to stay objective," Jessica said quietly, "even when it's a 'brother.' We can't suffer the child's every pain. The babies need us to keep functioning."

Emily breathed in deeply, exhaled, then nodded agreement. Trying to relegate her crisis to the past, she stood up.

"Good girl," Jessica also stood. "Where'll we put 'Lee'?"

Emily frowned. "Let...let me think about it."

15

Jessica moved toward Emily to hold her. The phone rang. Jessica thought it more important to hug Emily than answer immediately. She held her until her trembling stopped, then released her. "Talk to Joe Greeley," Jessica said. "See if there is a non-White home on his foster parent applicant list."

"I will."

"Thanks for being on top of it."

Emily nodded, smiled tenuously, and left the office.

Jessica picked up the phone. "Yes, Nancy."

"George Liebman on one."

"Tell him there are still no Jewish children."

"This is the third time he's called."

"Okay," Jessica said, annoyed at his insistence, "*I'll* tell him. Put him through." Jessica took a deep breath. "Yes, Mr. Liebman."

"It's been two years, Mrs. Keebler, since we put in our application…"

"There are still no Jewish children available, Mr. Liebman."

"We'll take a child of *any* national origin!" He was loud, angry, and impatient. "Any *race! Any color!*"

Stunned, Jessica took the phone from her ear and looked at it with her mouth open. *Did he have a bug to our meeting? Does he understand what he's saying? Or is it his frustration exploding?* Jessica continued to grapple with it silently.

Liebman quieted down as he explained. "Lil and I work with children of different races all the time. We wrote 'Jewish child' on our application because you said that asking for a child of like religion would facilitate the process."

Jessica, still working her way through shock, wasn't hearing him. She was trying to get past her disbelief. "You'll take a child…of *any* national origin?"

Liebman was silent. Jessica thought he'd already changed his mind, but heard him ask,

"I'm sorry?"

"You're willing to take a child of *any* national origin?"

"Yes, of course!"

16

"You're not just saying that…to speed up the process."

"No, I…we mean it."

Jessica debated whether to encourage him. *Will they follow through?* "Would you and your wife be willing to…to write *that* on your application?"

"Yes, happy to."

Jessica hesitated. "Tomorrow morning?"

"That would be fine."

"Nine-thirty? Ten?"

"Ten would work."

"Uh…fine…good. See you then."

"Thank you."

Slowly, Jessica lowered the phone, cradled it, but kept her hand on it while she tried to understand the sudden turbulence in her head. *Why did I tell him to change his application? Do I intend to go ahead with this?* Her hand came off the phone to her throbbing forehead. *Am I really thinking of offering him a mixed baby? What if Sacramento hears about this? Of course they'll hear about it. Then what?* She knew the pressure in her head was her blood pressure at a peak. Jessica dropped back in her chair, closed her eyes and took a deep breath. She held it until she felt uncomfortable and let it out. She repeated it until she had calmed herself somewhat. Opening her eyes, she smiled at the simplicity of what she was thinking. *It's such an instant solution. Solution? Yes, if they'd let mixed babies go to White homes.* "Even *they* can see that," she murmured, smiling ironically at her sudden, unlikely fantasy. *On a street of foster homes, all the doors swing open and the babies fly toward eager, waiting arms.* "If only, if only," she muttered cynically.

Jessica remembered her physician, Phyllis Coleman's, reiterated advice, *Take a break, Jessica, take a break. Stop carrying the weight of the world on your shoulders.* Jessica stood and stretched her arms high, breathing deeply. She exhaled fully, then repeated the exercise. "Keep the blood pressure down," she whispered to herself, "keep it down."

Back in her chair, she dropped her glasses to hang from the gold chain around her neck and rubbed her eyes. Replacing her glasses, she sat back to think. *Will Steve support me? I'll have to consult with his state office. They...they'll have to change the law.* Fearsome about where this was taking her, Jessica applied the brakes and stared intently at Emily's report on her desk blotter. *This is not an everyday-in-the-week memo I jot down for Steve. My God! It would have to go to the legislature before I can even move on it.*

"Whoa, back up, Jessica," she said aloud, "the Liebmans have yet to be processed. They may not qualify." She felt silly for having zoomed into thin space. *If they don't qualify, no need to talk to Sacramento, or anybody. We'll live, as usual, with what we have, Heaven help us.*

Jessica was determined not to lose the rest of her workday in the yes-and-no possibilities of her revolutionary idea.

The temptation, however, to deflate the unmanageable numbers of unadoptables back to the usual adoption volume, refused to be ignored. For the rest of the day, the bevy of pro-and-con bees buzzed her. She swatted them away so she could focus on the case reports she was reading, but uncertainty sneaked them back to demand an audience.

The word 'revolutionary' detoured Jessica's thinking to the student sit-in strike at UC Berkeley, where her son, Jonathon, had started his second year. With his passionate outbursts against what he considered social injustices, he was a likely activist in the student protest. But worrying about her son was not solving the agency problem. Determined to have her notes ready for use at Emily's next evaluation meeting, Jessica focused herself again on Emily's file.

Satisfied with her note-taking, she closed and filed Emily's and took out Grace's folder. But Jessica's mind would not clear of her other concerns. Looking at the clock, she saw the minute hand was past 4:30, on its way to five. She closed Grace's file and decided to leave. *'Sleep on it,'* Lenny used to say. *'It'll look different in the morning.'* Suddenly Jessica was very hungry and could smell the Swanson's Beef Stroganoff sizzling in her toaster-oven.

Chapter 2

Jessica closed the door of her two-bedroom house behind her and bent to the floor to pick up her mail that had come through the slot. She'd thought to put a box on the door to catch it, but decided that the bending and straightening was good exercise. *Should pick 'em up one at a time if I weren't so hungry.*

Straightening with the gathered items in her hand, relief she usually felt when she closed the door of her little house did not kick in. *A smell, a feeling, someone else is in the house.* Her internal alarms went off. Frozen against the door, her hand moving slowly sought the large brass knob behind her. Her ears strained for sounds. A rustling noise started, then stopped abruptly. Jessica gasped, held her breath and turned her head toward it. *It's in my bedroom. Should I run?* Her phone was in the living room, ten feet in front of her. *Call 911?* The noise again, this time longer. *Definitely from my bedroom.* Her hand slowly turned the knob behind her. She tried to open the door, but it was too difficult a position. She'd never noticed how firmly the weather stripping held it. Her inability to run on cue terrified her. If she turned around and pulled on it, he'd be sure to hear. Sudden laughter from the bedroom. *Oh my God, a madman!* She heard a muffled rattling of her bedroom phone dropped into its cradle. Jessica's only thought was to get out. She turned and pulled on the door. It didn't budge. In her terror she'd forgotten to turn the knob. A loud voice behind her yelled, "Hi, Mom!"

Jessica gasped, whirled and shrank fearfully against the door.

"Mom."

The word finally registered. Jessica saw her son, Jonathon, long black hair to his shoulders, the brilliant white of his teeth grinning at her, flashing white against his newly-bronzed skin. Jessica's faint voice struggled upward toward normalcy. "Why…why didn't you use the phone in your room?"

"My legs are burned. I used your cold cream."

Slowly Jessica straightened, went forward and hugged him. She was glad to smell her boy again in his unwashed clothes, tempered by the sweet smell of the cream.

Aware of his mother's body touching his, Jonathan eased away, but completed the embrace with his arms.

Returning to normal, Jessica was mother again. "Wel…come home, Jonathon," she said indecisively. She backed away and looked at him critically. "What are you doing here? The fall semester started."

"College is bullshit, Mom."

"Jonathon," she snapped, "you said you'd finish the second year and *then* decide…"

Jonathan threw up his hands. "I couldn't take it, Mom. Three hundred kids in the lecture hall, nobody gets to ask questions. Sometimes the professor doesn't even show, sends his assistant, sometimes a goddam' tape!"

"But you said…"

"I *know* what I said, but what's it for? If you do any thinking, Joe McCarthy calls you a Communist. So what's left to talk about? College in America is bullshit."

Jessica saw her son's anger turn his face a ruddier bronze. She worried about what he might have been involved in at school. *Is that why he's home?* "Were you…in on the Berkeley sit-ins?"

"Of course, Mom!"

"You…you weren't arrested, Jonathon, were you?" In her mind that would be such a negative for him, for his resume.

"No, we left before the fun started. My friend, Jimmy, was driving to LA. His mother has breast cancer. He needed company. I was glad to get out of there anyway."

Jessica studied her twenty-year-old son critically, anxiously. "So what are you going to do?"

Jonathan started unbuttoning his khaki shirt. "Take a shower and wash my clothes. We slept in his car last night." He indicated his bedroom. "I've got a backpack of dirty clothes in there. The washing machine's still working, isn't it?"

Jessica smiled at his evasion of her question. *We'll talk after dinner,* she determined. "Yes, it is. I'll make dinner. Are you hungry?"

"Starved," Jonathan said, walking toward his room.

"It'll be double on Swanson's Beef Stroganoff, Jonno. I wasn't expecting to cook for a guest." Jessica smiled at her slipping into the old pattern of using his boyhood nickname. His friends invented it because two syllables were easier to say than three.

"That's okay, Mom."

The oval butcher-block table just off the kitchen served as kitchen/dinette eatery. When her husband Lenny died four years ago, Jessica sold their three-bedroom house and bought a two-bedroom house in the same residential area of West LA. The smaller house meant no dining room, simpler eating arrangements and less house to keep clean. It suited her just fine.

Dinner seemed to have a calming effect on her son. He settled back in his chair and idly diddled crumbs with his fingers.

Jessica enjoyed his company. She smiled. "It's nice to have you home, Jonno only don't scare me the next time."

"Scare you?"

"Yes. I came home looking forward to a quiet, private evening and I hear someone rummaging in my bedroom. I'm a woman. I live alone. Remember? Do you know what went on in my head?"

"Oh...yeah...sorry."

"Next time tell me when you expect to be here."

"Yeah, I will." Still max-relaxed, slumped Jonathan returned to his inner thoughts and was silent.

Jessica had been more generous in her dinner preparations than she'd intended and used extra dishes to serve soup and a guacamole dip of avocado, yogurt and lime juice, because it was his favorite. The many dirty dishes remaining on the table didn't bother Jonathan at all.

Eating alone, Jessica didn't experience such table clutter. She expected Jonathon to respond to the mess with a semblance of cooperation, but he sat, idly pushing the crumbs, frowning as if deep within himself. Jessica suddenly felt foolish for having succumbed to the temptation of treating her prodigal son royally, even put upon as she eyed him enjoying the digestion of his best meal in days, oblivious of any responsibility. "Clear," Jessica said, using the code word that daily reminded him of his table chores while growing up.

Dragged back to reality from wherever his wishful magic carpet had carried him, Jonathan looked up. "Huh?"

"Clear."

"Oh...yeah." The pace of his getting up to his full five-ten was slow, reluctant.

Jonathon's unfolding of himself reminded Jessica how tall her son had grown and her old silent question returned. *How come? Lenny was five-six and I'm five-three.* Of course there wasn't an answer. She smiled slightly to him. "And then we'll talk."

As if interrupted in his inner meanderings, Jonathan stood still and looked at her. "What about?"

"This quarter for which you registered and paid and are not attending."

"Yeah." Jonathon carried dishes to the sink, returning to his old chore of rinsing and stacking the dishwasher.

Except for a rare staff meeting at her house, Jessica hadn't used the dishwasher since Jonathan left for Berkeley a year ago. "Don't run it until after we talk."

"Okay."

Returning to the table, he wiped the dampness of his hands on his jeans. "I came home to tell you, Mom, that I *have* made plans," he said, plopping down and languidly extending his long legs.

"You have?"

"Yeah."

Jessica waited. Jonathan seemed thoughtful. His head was down. She finally asked, "What are they?"

He smiled, sheepishly, Jessica thought. *He's feeling foolish about this, whatever it is.*

He looked up at her with his brown eyes. His mouth opened, but hesitated. "Uh… Jimmy and I are gonna do the hostel tour in Europe."

Jessica tensed. "You are?"

"Yes."

"Now?"

Jonathan looked at his mother, not understanding her question. "Of course, now, not next year."

"For how long?"

Jonathan shrugged. "A month or two. Maybe longer."

"It's October, heading into winter. You'll freeze. Europe is not LA."

"So we'll come home."

"In any case, I want you home in time to register for the next quarter."

"That's three months away. We'll be home."

"Two-and-a-half months. That's a promise. Look at me, Jonathan." She waited for him to face her directly. "That's a promise."

"Yeah."

"When did this happen?"

"While we were sitting in."

"Is Eleanor going with you?"

"Eleanor?"

The where-did-that-come-from look on Jonathon's face surprised Jessica...

At spring break in April, Jonathon brought the vivacious Eleanor home to introduce to Jessica. *Obviously,* Jessica worried, watching them needing no excuse to constantly laugh and hold each other, *Jonathan and Eleanor are emotionally locked into each other.* Jessica felt the need to say what she thought. "I think, you two, that it's not a good idea to plan to marry while you're still students. Wait until you know what you want to do with your life."

"Archaeologist," Eleanor replied instantly.

"Jonathon's interest is political science." Jessica looked at her son for confirmation. She hoped they'd see that those two careers would pull them in two directions.

"Was, Mom."

"Was?"

He burst out in anger. "McCarthy wants all federal workers and students who get government loans to sign a loyalty oath. What crap! Is this politics in America?..."

Remembering that conversation, Jessica looked at her son. "Maybe a six-month cooling-off period for you and Eleanor's a good idea."

"Yeah, we kind of talked about that."

"Oh." Relieved that they weren't rushing it, and that their decision showed a maturity she hadn't given him credit for, "That's wise, Jonathan." She smiled inwardly. *Things change fast with young people.* She needed to know about his trip plans. "Just you and Jimmy going?"

"Yeah, when he knows the results of his mom's biopsy."

Jessica looked at Jonathan. "What if…"

Jonathan's impatient gesture interrupted her. It said he didn't want to think about that negative possibility. Swinging one arm, he swiped the subject away, saying, "We'll see, we'll see."

Jessica decided to leave it there, then debated whether to tell him about the new development, *possible new development,* she corrected herself, *at the agency.* She knew it would bounce her up to his wavelength. In her own way, she'd seem to be sharing his anti-establishment social concerns.

Jonathon started to get up.

"Your mother isn't behind the times either."

He looked at her. "Oh?"

"I told you about the California law that says racially-mixed babies may be given only to Negro families."

"Yeah, you did. It's a stupid, racist law."

"I think so too."

"But you're stuck with it, can't fight it 'cause that's where your paycheck comes from."

"*Our* paycheck, Jonathan," Jessica snapped. She was suddenly resentful of his forgetting her role in keeping him in the lifestyle to which he was accustomed. "My paycheck is what's sending you to college and to Europe, if you go."

Surprised by her angry tone, he waited. He saw his mother grin slyly.

"Maybe I can fight the stupid law," she said.

Jonathan gestured and spoke with heavy sarcasm. "Oh, you're gonna caravan your staff to the Sacramento legislature, sit in and shout, 'You're a bunch of racists. Change the law.'"

Jessica smiled. "No, Jonathan, I've got an unexpected ally. A White family has asked for a baby of *any* national origin."

Jonathon looked at her for a moment. Obviously he hadn't thought of that as a possibility. "Really?"

Jessica nodded. "Yes."

"But you can't..." Jonathan interrupted himself. "Can you?"

"Well, not legally."

"So?"

Jessica shrugged, but was silent. Thinking about what she'd just said, she realized she'd leaked the still classified information to impress her son, to build her rapport with him. Looking at him she knew she'd succeeded.

He was smiling. "What're you gonna do, Mom?"

Jessica smiled. His voice sounded as if he'd watch for the outcome to the last whistle. There was even a touch of awe in his tone. She playfully threw the ball to him, cementing their alliance. "What do *you* think I ought to do?"

Asked to be a problem solver instead of a denouncer crossed Jonathan's wires. He sputtered incomplete starts. His face reddened. "Yeah...well...I think I'd....maybe..."

"Pretend you're the director of the agency, Jonathan."

"Yeah."

Jessica grinned. He was in with her. She enjoyed having his attention, and pressed her points as mother, teacher, staff-trainer. "And you have the opportunity to give a mixed baby to a White family, but there's a law against it. What would you do?"

Jonathan looked at his mother standing there, smiling at him, teasing. "Yeah, yeah, I'd do it, Mom."

"Just like that?" she asked.

"Yeah."

"You have an assistant to consult…to convince…she may not agree with you, a supervisor at the state capitol who may disagree, or, if he agrees, has to ask the political structure of the state to change the law…"

"That's bullshit!"

Jessica laughed. "Life's a lot of BS, Jonathan. Learn how to cope with it."

He flung his hands up in frustration. "That's why I changed my mind about Poly Sci. It ain't worth it."

Jessica was silent. She felt she had to inject herself into his turbulence, help him, perhaps, take his BS by the horns. "Now that it isn't Poly Sci, what will it be?"

Jonathan quieted, became thoughtful. "I don't know, Mom."

"Pick a good one."

"Yeah." He nodded. "Yeah, Mom."

After a pause, Jessica spoke quietly. "Sleep on it. I've got a big day tomorrow." She stood up. "Run the dishwasher and get a good night's sleep."

He looked up and smiled thinly. "Yeah."

"I leave at eight-fifteen. Maybe we could have breakfast…" She remembered then that with no classes to go to, he wouldn't open his eyes before ten. They both smiled at the improbability. "I guess not. Good night, son. See you at dinner tomorrow."

"Yeah. 'Night, Mom."

Chapter 3

The Liebman phone call gave Jessica another restless night. She lay alone, staring into the dimness of her bedroom. Without realizing it, she put out her hand to feel for Lenny, as if hoping to ask his opinion as she'd done for twenty-eight years of their marriage. Although her smile was sad thinking of him, she felt glad that her stabbing pain of his loss had dulled enough to be taken out of the 'Continuing-Crisis' category and transferred to 'Past Hard-Knocks.'

Jessica was debating bringing her assistant, Roberta Walker, in on the possibilities sparked by the Liebman call. *Or should I wait?* Lenny would say, "Too soon. You're a big girl now. Explore it for a bit by yourself. When you know what you want Roberta to do, call her in."

Jessica thought about Lerny's imagined response. *Yes,* she agreed, *wait, because straitlaced Roberta could say, 'No, Jessica, I want no part of it', and stop me cold.*

Looking in the mirror in the morning, Jessica decided to deal with the darkened shadows under her eyes by doing extra time with the crushed-ice pack. The cold shock was also the alarm bell demanding she start her day. Jessica decided to go in early. *I need thinking time to be very sure of my decision.*

She parked outside the agency at eight-fifteen instead of five-to-nine. Grateful for LA's brilliant sunshine bouncing heat waves off the forty-two brick steps, warming up the chill October morning, she climbed toward the heavy glass doors of the entrance. Inside it was comforting to see Nancy already at the switchboard adjusting her headset to do the least flattering of her wavy hairdo.

"Morning, Nancy."

"Morning, Jessica. You're early."

"Yep."

In her office Jessica opened the Liebman file. *Dance teachers, both of them. How much income can they have? Hippies?* The information left her shaking her head. She sat back in her chair. *This may not work at all. Questions will fly hot and heavy. If the parent safetey margin is questionable as well, I'll never get this through the eye of the needle.*

Jessica closed the Liebman file and sat back shaking her head again. *Yet, of the hundreds of White families who have utilized the agency, this is the first one offering to accept an inter-racial child. Are the Liebmans weirdos? Intellectual liberals? Communists?*

Jessica thought of last evening's discussion with Jonathon. She imagined him leaning across the breakfast table, political passion heating his face red, moistening his brown eyes, and hitting the table with his fist, saying, *'Do it, Mom! Show the racist bastards!'* Jessica smiled. She understood her son's intensity. She felt as deeply about her babies as he did about politics.

She leaned forward and opened the file again. *The Liebmans have two girls. Only one lives with them...second marriage for both of them...is the present marriage stable? They do own their own house. Mortgage payments, $128 a month, minimal. How much of a house can it be? Is it adequate?*

Jessica leaned back again. A lot of questions had to be answered. *Will Roberta be willing to go ahead in a case like this and do a home visit? I do need to talk to her.* Jessica looked at her watch. Five-to-nine. She picked up the phone. "Roberta, please, Nancy...Morning, Roberta, got a minute?...Yes, now if you can...Thanks."

The quiet knock on her door followed by a moment of silence reminded Jessica of Roberta's diligently pursued proprieties. Anyone else on staff would have knocked and barged in. Jessica smiled and shook her head. *Two years with the agency and her Emily Post manners still surprise me. Yet she's as conscientious and devoted a social worker as she is proper.* "Come in, Roberta."

Roberta opened the door. "Good morning, Jessica."

Jessica smiled, nodded and gestured to the chair alongside her desk.

"Thank you."

Jessica noted Roberta's light gray suit with the ruffled pink blouse showing between the lapels. *No cleavage, of course.* Two years in LA from the Kansas State Agency, but Roberta did not let herself relax into the casual dress wear of sunny California. Jessica's multi-colored dirndl skirt, white blouse and embroidered vest seemed florid by comparison. But Jessica liked the way her outfit brightened up her gray-haired look. She preferred colors in her clothing to coloring her hair. And just a suggestion of cleavage, *femininely necessary. Or is it because it's four years since Lenny died?*

Sitting close, Jessica noted Roberta's permed coiffure, every hair in place. *That's it. Despite the extraordinary caseload she carries, Roberta is every hair in place.* Jessica thought of the Liebman offer requiring a breaking of the rules to complete. *Will it dishevel Roberta? Get me a flat No? Yet how else go ahead but ask her?*

After fumbling words silently, Jessica said, "I'm just going to dive into this, Roberta."

Roberta's gray eyes behind perfectly cleaned lenses sprang to alert.

"We have an opportunity, Roberta," Jessica slowed down to avoid any misunderstanding, "to give a mixed child to a White family."

Roberta's eyes widened.

Alarm? Condemnation? Probably both, Jessica decided. She nodded vigorously. "I know the law, Roberta, but for the sake of argument…no, for the sake of our agency's *vision,* let's say we can unlock the door confining these babies to foster homes, questionable homes at that, and instead, put them into permanent placement, which is our function. Doesn't the regulation preventing that from happening seem archaic?"

Roberta's long silence was an agony for Jessica. *I can't attempt this alone, certainly not without my assistant who's privy to all my professional thoughts.*

When Roberta finally spoke, it was in a voice so low Jessica had to lean forward to hear. "You…are compromising me, Jessica, as you are yourself, if you go ahead with this…"

Jessica's repeated vigorous nodding interrupted her. "I know that, Roberta, but I…I cannot go ahead…without your agreement."

That last phrase was a rifle shot that snapped Roberta back in her chair to sit up even straighter. She took a long time to respond, with a quiet, but clear annoyance in her tone. "I don't like going outside regulations, Jessica."

"I know that, Roberta." *No kidding,* was Jessica's sarcastic thought, but it was not the time to be snippy. Instead, she repeated quietly, "I know that, Roberta. I spent a sleepless night debating whether to involve you in this or not."

Roberta sat more stiffly than before, looking as if she'd frozen herself out of further communication on the subject. "I need time, Jessica, to think about this." Roberta leaned forward slightly as if to get up.

I need resolution, Jessica decided. She didn't want Roberta to leave without a go-ahead. Jessica touched the file on her desk. "This is the Liebman file, the Caucasian family that expressed an interest in a child of 'any national origin.' That's as far as it's gone. There's been no commitment, no acceptance of any kind on our part. It's our move. They may not qualify, or they may. A single house visit will tell us. As an adoptive family they will be judged by our standards. If they don't qualify, the matter is dropped and we live with what we have." Jessica looked at Roberta to see if she was having any effect.

Jessica decided to stop there. She sat back into the cushion-soft support of her high-backed chair and exhaled to lessen her tension. Waiting, she picked up her pen, rolled it to different positions with her fingers. She waited for anything from Roberta, but Roberta was silent, her discomfort obvious.

Roberta was reeling internally. She'd respected, often admired Jessica for her handling of one difficult crisis after another. Roberta had settled into feeling safe in following Jessica's leadership in everything until …this… Roberta's comfort mold was violently shaken, bringing tears to her eyes.

Her assistant's glistening eyes signaled Jessica to back off. She waited until she thought of a compromise that would not violate her assistant. "Roberta," she started quietly, "without your subscribing to any infraction of the rules…vulnerability on that score would be mine alone… one house visit. Would you be willing to take it that far?"

Roberta sat stiffly in her hot seat, so obviously miserable, Jessica felt pity for her. To make it doubly clear that Roberta would, in no way, be touched with blame by her supervisor's infraction, Jessica repeated, "The responsibility will be no one's but mine in this, Roberta." Jessica stopped to let that sink in. "As you would with any client, would you be willing to do the home visit, check finances, etcetera, *without any responsibility* for *my* unorthodox decision?"

Jessica waited again to be sure her points were understood. "You are only asked to do your usual job of caseworker gathering the usual information."

During another long wait, Jessica managed a surreptitious glance at her watch. Ten-to-ten. She hoped the Liebmans wouldn't be on time. *Better if Roberta doesn't get the impression that I'd determinedly gone ahead with this without her acceptance.*

Roberta cleared her throat and spoke each word as if revealing missing diamonds one by one, secretly hidden in her care. "If…I do agree…to doing the interviews, it doesn't mean, Jessica, that I agree to your new ruling."

"No, Roberta. I take sole and full responsibility for that. I'm simply asking you to do an adoptive parent check on a new applicant."

Roberta, lips pursed tensely, dissected each word of Jessica's last statement, then spent the next minutes forming the words of her response. "All right, Jessica, just…*only*… the one interview." She stood up quickly, anxious to leave.

Relieved, grateful, Jessica understood that she'd dumped a lot on her assistant, disrupting Roberta's way of handling her life. Standing with an effusive, "Thank you, Roberta," she reached impulsively and embraced her.

Stunned by the touching, Roberta stood wooden.

Jessica felt Roberta's tension of fear and eased her arms from enthusiastic to gentle. Roberta smelled faintly of pleasant fragrance. "Thank you, Roberta," Jessica whispered, "for trusting me."

Slowly Roberta's arms came up to tentatively complete the embrace because that's what one is supposed to do. She whispered in turn, "You're welcome, Jessica." She dropped her arms, left quickly and closed the door.

Drained, Jessica dropped into her chair. Elbow on the arm support, she rested her aching forehead on her hand. *And this is only the beginning. What did it do to my blood pressure?* She sat up to touch two fingers to her wrist pulse...*ragged...and too fast.* She shook her head. *Overdo the tension, Jessica, and Dr. Coleman will have you back on medication.* She stood up, stretched her arms toward the ceiling and breathed deeply. It felt so good to stretch. *I must remember to do this....*

The knock on the door interrupted her. She dropped her arms and straightened her vest. "Come in."

The door opened and the Liebman couple came in, the woman noticeably shorter than the man. It was two years since Jessica had seen them. *Oh, yes,* she thought, remembering them, *the dancers.* Both gave the appearance of standing unusually straight and exuded a youthful energy, *though...almost...forty? But of course, they're dancers.* Dressed California casual, he, in pale blue slacks and open-collared shirt, she, in embroidered white blouse and full tan skirt. *Not kooks...not hippies...hopeful, hopeful.* Smiling, Jessica advanced with outstretched hand toward the man. "Nice to see you again, Mr. Liebman." They shook hands. "And Mrs. Liebman." The wife's grip was as firm as his. Jessica gestured toward the two chairs in front of her desk. "Please have a seat." Jessica moved around the desk to her chair and all sat.

Jessica found the application sheet in the thin file and turned it toward them. "This is your original application." She index-fingered the proper space. "Here, change the wording to 'any national origin'." Jessica handed him her pen.

Liebman carefully ran three lines through 'Jewish' and printed in the required phrase below it. He laid the pen on the desk and sat up grinning.

Jessica smiled and looked at his wife. She was frowning slightly as if thinking hard.

"What's next?" Liebman asked.

"A home visit. Your social worker, Miss Walker, will call you for an appointment."

"Thank you." The Liebmans got up to leave.

Jessica sent them off with a "Thank you for coming in."

She turned the application to double-check what he'd written, reinserted it into the folder and closed it. She opened the right-hand bottom drawer of her desk, placed it alphabetically into the active file and closed it. She took a deep breath, let it out, rested her elbows on the desk and her head on her hands. Her comfortable little house in West LA beckoned. Jessica wished it were the end of the day, but it had just begun.

Chapter 4

George Liebman was jubilant as he and his wife, Lil, pushed open the glass doors of the agency and stepped out into warm LA sunshine. "Wow, we should've done that long ago."

"Yes," Lil agreed, "two years wasted."

They started down the long ramp of steps toward the sidewalk. "Live and learn," she added. Four years ago Lillian felt the urgency of having a child to steady their turbulent marriage. George was surprised at Lil's insistence. Their lives were busy with teaching and maintaining a dance studio and raising Lil's daughter, Amy. Eventually George agreed to having another child, but two tubal pregnancies in two years, ended their natural possibilities. Lil talked adoption. George checked the Jewish agency. No Jewish children were available. They registered with the LA County Bureau of Adoptions.

Though reacting to Lil's pressure, George had come to look forward to having a child. He hoped to be a more successful father than he'd been so far. After a boring six-year first marriage, George and his ex-wife, Rachel, agreed to separate at the end of World War II when George would no longer be needed for war production at the Westinghouse plant outside Philadelphia. V-Day was more than an ecstatic welcoming of the armistice. Rachel discovered she was pregnant. Westinghouse compounded George's chaos by offering to train him as a jet-propulsion engineer, when George was hoping to leave the industry to pursue his interest in theater.

The jet-propulsion engineer position guaranteed a salary for life, economic stability that George had never known as an adult. Yet having successfully weathered ten years of the Depression and strategically strengthened a branch of war production for four years, George, arrogantly, had no fear of the economic unknown, and didn't

34

feel the need to plan ahead.

After the war, George signed on as a machinist with Union Pacific Railroad to get free transportation to Los Angeles, where he hoped to contact New York theater friends who'd also migrated to LA. He wrote to Rachel that he would bring her and baby Donna to LA, and would see them well settled before proceeding with the divorce.

Baby Donna hardly felt welcomed in the world of separated parents, nor could she bond with a father whose parental visits were sporadic. In LA George divided his time between machinist work and evening experiments in theater. This serendipity of living each day seemed normal to one who'd been kicked out of college by the Depression after only one semester. He'd survived by his wits for seven years and his creative understanding of machines catapulted him to guru status of industrial importance in war production.

After the war, at age 29, George still had the bounding energy of youth and the arrogance of successful-at-whatever-I-put-my-hand-to. This son of the depression had learned that without planning, he'd be a success at whatever came along. This no-plan-for-the-future, survival-for-one pattern provided no nourishing stability for his daughter, and left George unfulfilled as a father. At the point of adopting, he had the many haunting regrets of an unsuccessful parent. The adoption could give him another shot at being a nourishing father.

When George and Lil sat down to dinner that night, they told twelve-year-old Amy, they had changed their adoptive request to a child of any national origin, to improve their chances of getting one.

Near-teen Amy, already challenging her parents, turned her blue eyes on George, then Lil. Neither her biological father nor her present family were observant Jews. "Why did you put down Jewish in the first place?" she questioned them critically.

"The agency told us to," Lil explained, "because their policy is to give a Jewish child to a Jewish family, a Catholic child to a Catholic family. They said we'd get one more quickly."

Amy trained three times a week at her parents' *Dance Center* with a mix of Chicano, Anglo, Negro and Jewish students. Her neighborhood junior high was a similar blend. When they had discussed the adoption with her, she'd been comfortable with 'any kind of baby' as a brother or sister. Living the last nine years with two busy parents, she was an only child, hungry for some child talk and child play in the house. She had felt the two-year delay as keenly as they. "Why didn't you put down 'any kind of child'?"

Lil's blue eyes smiled at her daughter's. "We did, Amy. That's just what we did."

The Liebman gears at the agency, spider-webbed in idleness for two years, but powered now by the director's courageous decision, creaked off dead center. Roberta Walker phoned the Liebmans the next morning, introduced herself, and asked for an appointment to visit their house on the Echo Park hillside of Los Angeles.

"Great," said George, "when would you like to make it?"

"Is today possible?"

George thought quickly. *Wednesday. I don't teach, but Lil does.* "Do we both have to be here?"

"No, it's mostly a house visit. As long as one of you is there."

"Good." George did need time to go around and pick up the usual mess. "This afternoon," he said, "around one or two?"

"One-thirty?"

"That's fine."

George gave Miss Walker directions how to find the corner of Echo park Avenue from Sunset Boulevard, then described the winding road that was Lakeshore Avenue. "Stay with it until you get to Ewing Street on your left. Ewing Street is only fifty yards long, in a cul-de-sac. Pull in there and park. I've cut a driveway up to our house on the left, but don't drive up. It's not finished yet. Walk up the steps."

After George hung up, Miss Walker's words, 'house visit,' reverberated in his head. *A check to see if the house is adequate, if we have a decent place to live. Oh no! Not only don't we have space yet for another child...* George interrupted his thoughts to look around, this time with the critical eyes of an agency worker. A thirty-five-year-old cracker-box of a house that Lil bought during the war for eighteen hundred dollars.

Fortunately, knowing they would have to add a bedroom to be granted a child, George had begun the process of enlarging what had been built in 1920 as a summer shack. He'd asked Hank, a contractor friend, to draw up plans for two more bedrooms and a deck with steps leading down to a driveway-to-be-built. But at the imminence of Miss Walker's visit, the bedrooms were only blueprints.

George's fears focused on the most sub-standard feature of the house, Amy's Alcove. George walked into the six-by-eight nook off the living room that Amy slept in, small and dark with a crudely-hinged window on the side wall. The high side of her steeply-slanted shed roof was hung from the house. The room spoke of a chicken coop cleaned up in the distant past and quickly improvised into a sleeper for an unplanned-for child, by two kids unversed in birth control.

George wished it had already been demolished as the plans indicated, but it was still Amy's bedroom. He turned to look at the main area, the living room. He and Lil slept at the far end of the living room. In the morning they straightened the bedclothes, threw a lot of cushions on it and called it a divan, studio style. An open deck the length of the house occupied the Ewing Street side and a small kitchen and bath at the other end completed the rectangle.

How do I explain the condition of the house to validate the adoption request? Pressure-cooked by the imminent house visit, George silently replayed the progress on the remodel. Having it all at his fingertips would make his telling of the projected plans more plausible. He and Hank discovered that the four-by-fours supporting the house didn't rest on concrete piers, but on wooden mud sills that termites had dined on thoroughly. He and Lil couldn't afford to contract a new foundation *and* the bedrooms. To do the foundation himself, George rented a small bulldozer and cut a curving roadway from the cul-de-sac below up to the house, to enable him to bring in materials to work on the foundation.

The old posts and mud sills gone, two two-by-twelves on end under the main joists, resting on jacks, temporarily supported the house. Outside, stacked concrete blocks, bags of cement, and mounds of sand and gravel looked promising. *If Miss Walker has any imagination, the blueprints will tell her about the rest of the remodel. Is there enough here to convince her our request is justified? Space enough for another child? The porch! The porch!* George suddenly remembered the problem at the entrance. He rushed out the back door and down to the cellar for hammer and nails, rushed back up to the front of the house and reinforced the plywood square on the porch covering the hole where he'd torn out rotted wood. *We don't want Miss Walker falling through to the cellar.* Expecting Lil home for lunch, George washed his hands and made a tuna salad.

When he and Lil sat down to eat, George told her about Miss Walker coming at one-thirty. Lil was indignant that he was having their first meeting without her. "That's when I leave to teach."

"I know, Lil. I told her you had to work. She said this is only a house visit, only one of us needs be here. She just wants to see if there's going to be room for the baby."

"There isn't yet. What did you tell her?"

"What I *will* tell her is that we're planning two bedrooms and a deck, and I'll show her the blueprints, and, of course, the new foundation. Everything you and I have talked about so far."

Lil looked past George through the window to the cul-de-sac below. "Is that her?"

George turned and looked. A white coupe was parked in front of Lil's car. A slim, blue-suited woman was walking toward the steps. Her purse hung from her shoulder and she carried a thin brief-case. "Probably." George bounced up, put the dishes in the sink and wiped down the table. Rinsing the sponge, he looked critically at the sink. The worn porcelain under the hot water spigot had formed a crack that wiggled its way to the steel drain. The edges of the crack had chipped and yellowed. It reminded George yet again how flimsy and inadequate the house was, one of the many things that didn't usually bother him until he adopted critical agency vision. *The sink's gotta be changed, but bedrooms first. I hope she'll understand.*

Roberta Walker put her hand on the two-inch pipe banister and looked up at the long tier of cement steps the city had built to provide walking passage from the Ewing Street cul-de-sac up to Alvarado Street on the ridge of the hill. The metal banister was not unpleasantly cold to touch as she'd expected, but warm from the Los Angeles sun. Miss Walker smiled. *Fall weather in Kansas isn't like this.* She looked up at the house sitting to the left of the steps. *Cute, quaint.* The faded coat of paint might have once been yellow. *God, I hope it's adequate.* She looked around at the dried weeds of the neglected hillside, the rocky mix of dirt and sandstone parched to thirsty tan. *There's so much riding on this application; the private, secretive conference with Jessica. Jessica's repeated warning not to say anything to anyone yet, outside or inside the agency. The Liebman possibility.* Two clumps of tall cane offered their leaves to a tepid breeze. *No expensive landscaping here; everything casual in LA. If something dreadful happens to the baby here, if they divorce six months after getting the baby...* Miss Walker shook her head as she climbed, then turned left on the dirt path to the house. A row of cane clumps in a crude circle screened a patio roughed out of the sandstone. *We do have too many mixed babies and the Liebmans are the only family who offered...* She stopped to look at the house built on the narrow flat. The left side, to the roof line, rose twenty feet vertically from the unfinished driveway below. On the right, a narrow access path to the back had been picked out of the sandstone. *Whether they'd have enough money to finalize the adoption is questionable. Can they spare the two hundred dollars? If it ever gets to the final papers.*

Roberta's fifteen years of social work in Kansas had qualified her for her mid-level job in LA. She was pleased to be the professional confidante of the director, yet she resented the burden Jessica laid on her of knowingly ignoring agency guidelines. *Jessica's got a brainstorm. Not that she's wrong. We do have a crisis.*

George and Lil waited outside on the open porch for Miss Walker who was on the dirt path crossing the patio. George thought the plywood repair looked tacky but he was satisfied that it was sturdy.

He and Lil shook hands with Miss Walker, traded the pleasant words of introduction and ushered her into the house. Lil wore a thin sweater and skirt over her leotard and tights. She apologized for having to leave to teach.

"I understand," Miss Walker said, primly but not unpleasantly. Lil left.

George felt relieved. Lil hadn't had the patience to sit through the short and long term construction planning with Hank. *If Lil were here, I'd have to explain once to her for her okay, and then repeat it to Miss Walker.* Yet, without Lil, George had to prove that the house, despite its present state, would eventually be adequate for another child. *I could use some of Lil's driving will.*

George remained near the door. Miss Walker walked to the center of the living room. She turned to see the large divan with throw-over spread and cushions at the patio end, then turned to see the kitchen at the other end. She stood before George in her light blue business suit and shell-pink blouse. Her small regular features were tastefully accented with a touch of pink lipstick and cheek blush. Light blue eyes behind the spotless glasses looked critically at the ceiling and walls.

George, in T-shirt, slacks and sandals felt the difference of their two worlds. *No way, in her eyes, is this will-do house adequate. Does this lady have the imagination, looking at blueprints, to understand what the eventual space will be? This fair-skinned, impeccable-looking lady could pass a harsh judgement on our California cottage; cute at best, sub-standard at worst.*

Miss Walker's mouth seemed more tightly pursed than since she'd entered. *Her professional, judgemental look of disapproval?* George wondered.

Knowing he'd be under the gun to prove the adequacy of their place when he showed Miss Walker around, George knew their family situation would also come under scrutiny. Waiting for her to initiate the next steps, George silently argued for the honesty of their lifestyle as if he were responding to her probing questions. *Lil and I don't require luxurious furnishings. What few dollars we have after the*

*food and bills, we spend on music, costumes, teaching, performing.
We're busy with the development of students, parents, our board,
and making Dance Center a success. Our cultural outreach to the
community is our focus. The house is adequate for our resting, eating
and privacy for love-making needs.*

Having prepared the statement, George hoped she'd give him a
chance to say it.

She was still standing in the center of the living room. George
thought to move things along. He opened the front door that connected
the porch entrance directly to the living room, to explain that the
planned enclosure of the porch that would turn it into living space.
He pointed to a stack of large wood-framed windows on the porch,
leaning against the outside of the house that he'd bought at a second-
hand yard. "They'll be glass walls on two sides of the porch, letting
in lots of light."

Though Miss Walker nodded in response to his explanations,
George was having a hard time getting past her super WASP
appearance. Remembering Mrs. Keebler's stunned response to his
unusual adoption request, he wondered why she would assign such
an obviously proper woman of traditional values to oversee the
agency's groundbreaking adoption.

Miss Walker's ill-fitting conventional presence in his
unconventional aura reminded George, yet again, that he lived as a
contrarian. It could not have been more clearly stated than in the
juxtaposition of the two, Miss Walker and George Liebman. Ever
since he'd been subordinated to his dominating older brother, from
his first yowl at being pushed into the world, George felt the need to
leap away from what everyone else did and create something
different, no matter if it was risky, and it usually was.

Watching Miss Walker scan his living quarters made George
realize that 'risk' and its siblings, 'different' and 'creative,' were the
norms in his life, had been, and were. During the few minutes it took
to show Miss Walker the present house, his mind raced on to capture
and comprehend the many ingredients in his current and past lives
kicked loose by their adoption request. The prospect of being under

scrutiny as to who he was, brought up his role in the war, the dominance of his brother, difficulties between his mother and father, his decision to turn down Westinghouse's offer to train him as an engineer, fleeing job and career stability for some unknown magic in Los Angeles. *Nineteen-thirty-eight!* He'd hitch-hiked from New York and spent three days in LA when it felt like a western cowtown under the bluest of skies, and spent ten days in northern California working for Leslie Blades in San Luis Obispo, who asked George to stay and work with him rehabilitating juvenile delinquents through a farm way of life. *Yes, I did fall in love with those clearest blue skies I'd ever seen and the dry warmth of California in August.* George cautioned himself not to bring up these items, which were irrelevant to the adoption. *Yes, big events in my life, but nothing to do with the adoption or Miss Walker. She'll think me a garrulous idiot if I drop an autobiography on her.*

His life under question for the adoption of a baby, George again watched Miss Walker make her silent observations. *Well,* he conceded, *the establishment has to know the child will be safe, and have opportunities to grow. Mrs. Keebler sent a lady like Miss Walker who's obviously concerned for the necessary traditional standards.*

Suddenly the adoption, if it depended on conforming to establishment rules, seemed shaky to the contrarian. George's stomach felt queasy.

"What are you planning for the bedrooms, Mr. Liebman?"

George gestured to the free-form, bean-shaped table top, bolted along its center line to a horizontal, supporting beam, so one side was in the kitchen, the other in the living room. He'd left the blueprints on it in preparation for her visit. They sat on the living room side of the table, but George immediately stood to unroll the blueprints. He recovered his enthusiasm as he launched into his explanation of the construction plan.

When Miss Walker seemed to understand the scope of the additions, he outlined the work sequence. "The foundation and cellar floor first, then the bedrooms."

Miss Walker nodded. "How long do you think it will take you to complete the bedrooms?"

"Once we get on them, two to three weeks."

Miss Walker calculated silently. "And the foundation and cellar?"

"Three to four weeks."

Again she went silent, then nodded. "I think the timing will work." She looked directly at George. "If you complete it on schedule."

George affirmed with a nod. "We'll do our best."

Miss Walker took legal-length forms out of her brief case. "I have to ask you about yours and Mrs. Liebman's joint income."

George nodded to show her that was agreeable, but as he rolled up the blueprints and put them aside, behind his brave façade his stomach dove for the pits again. *Money? We have just enough, but not according to her standards.*

Miss Walker filled in some blanks on the first sheet, passed it behind the others and filled in blanks on the second sheet. She passed the second behind the others, tapped the stack on end to even it out and laid it down.

In the long silence George was racing through some economic facts that he knew would be crucial for the agency's 'yay' or 'nay' to the adoption. *Joint income* reminded him that the IRS had sent a notice to their tax accountant, Marshal, that the Liebmans were to be audited. The Feds accused the Liebmans of making more money than their stated $6,000 annual gross. George had laughed cynically at the news. *I wish.* In preparation for the audit, Marshal had George itemize their monthly expenses backed up by receipts and copies of checks to prove that they really lived as frugally as their small annual income forced them to.

Grappling with preparation for Miss Walker's anticipated questions, George realized their problems with the adoption agency were exactly opposite to those they had with the Feds. With the Feds, they had to prove $6,000 a year *was* enough to support a family of three even though the IRS disagreed. Specifically, the IRS rejected their budget breakdown of eleven dollars a week for food. George recalled the IRS notice, '*No family of three can feed itself on that. You have income you're not declaring.*'

Sitting opposite Miss Walker, George had a moment of memory clarity that made him sweat. *The audit notice came soon after the visit by the FBI!* ...

Two men had knocked on the door one morning, showed their IDs and said, "Federal Bureau Of Investigation." One asked, "Can we come in and talk?"

"No," George answered, "we can talk right here."

One pulled out two eight-by-ten headshots from a manila envelope. George recognized two youngsters who'd been in the Youth Drama Group he'd directed the previous year. "Would you identify them for us?" the agent said.

"Why?" George asked.

"We think they're Communists."

"McCarthy's committee was closed down by the Senate last year. The hearings are over."

"The Communists are still a danger."

"What danger?" George replied. "Ten people sitting around, talking about the evils of Capitalism? Every college has a course on Marx's *Das Kapital*. Will you put the colleges on your un-American list?"

The agent indicated the photos. "You won't identify them?"

"No."

The agent put the photos back in the envelope and they left.

Two months later, Marshal, the Liebman's accountant, phoned them to say they were going to be audited.

Joe McCarthy's hearings struck deeply into LA's cultural community. Beyond Hollywood, it scorched grass roots cultural activities around the city. Bella Lewitsky, partner in Lester Horton's *Dance Theater* on Melrose Avenue, had been subpoenaed to testify, to name names of Communists she knew. On the stand she said, "I'm a dancer, not a singer."

She was applauded for her courage, but the blacklist of starring actors, writers, and directors dictated movieland's hiring for the next ten years. The oppressive anti-Communist smog continued to smother cultural activities in LA after McCarthy's committee was finally dethroned, and small people, like the Liebmans, whose classes and performances involved all ethnic groups and whose orbit occasionally touched Hollywood's, were beset with annoying legal obstacles like tax auditing.

Miss Walker was straightening out the stack of papers again by tapping the end on the table. She laid it down and picked up her pen. "Gross annual income?"

"$6,000."

Miss Walker wrote.

Her control is extraordinary, George thought. *She didn't shake her head in pity, or look at me as if she hadn't heard right.*

The rest of her questions ferreted out property taxes, mortgage and insurance payments, clothing costs, maintenance costs of their two cars and health plan arrangements. "And what do you estimate your food budget is for the week?"

George stared at her as if turned to stone. The adoption agency would eventually check their tax return. If he upped the figure he'd be caught in a lie. "Eleven dollars a week." George saw the look on her face. "That was last year," he explained. "We're doing better this year. I had more twenty-five dollar bookings for square-dance calling and folk-dance teaching. It's probably up to fifteen or sixteen a week this year."

Miss Walker nodded, and jotted numbers on the sheet.

Fearing the unbearable 'No' to their adoption request, George held his breath. Miss Walker's fingers were rolling the ballpoint pen one way, then back, squeezing so hard the skin over her knuckles was taut and white. *Is she finding the adoption impossible?*

George did a quick mental rundown of their finances as Miss Walker had picked them over. *No way those minimum amounts qualify for an adoption.* George countered the anticipated result with a verbal explanation. "We live frugally, Miss Walker. Lil and I shop at the public market downtown once a week where things are much cheaper. We can fruits and vegetables in season, and I raise chickens and rabbits in the back yard to supplement our food budget."

The pen stopped rolling. She looked at George. "You raise

chickens and rabbits?"

"Yes, I'd like to show them to you."

"I'd like to see them."

"Good." George waited till she gathered her papers, put them in her brief case, and snapped it shut. Apparently, that part of the interview was over. George talked as he led the way through the kitchen. He flinched, knowing she'd see the yellowed condition of the sink, but he carried on. "The chickens are Rhode Island Reds, and the rabbits, New Zealand Whites." In the closet-like space off the kitchen that housed the hot water heater, they skirted the domed metal hood of the chick brooder. "This is where I brood the chicks until they're big enough to put outside."

Miss Walker nodded.

Standing outside the back door in the bright sun, George decided not to risk her safety on the steep path to the chicken and rabbit cages at the bottom corner of the hillside lot. The rock steps he'd built close to the back of the house leading down to the cellar were also too irregular for her to chance. Instead, George pointed to the coop and hutches at the far corner. "There they are."

Miss Walker nodded. "Yes."

"The eggs are wonderful."

Her second yes had a touch of enthusiasm. It encouraged George to delineate for Miss Walker the transformation he'd accomplished in the ample back yard from dead-weed hillside to terraced strips of land supporting young fruit trees. With remembered excitement of their trip to the terraced fields of the Indians in the high mountains of Central Mexico, George told Miss Walker that he'd gotten the idea for terracing his steep wasteland of a back yard from the Indians in Mexico's mountains. He enumerated the tangerine, cherry, apricot and pear trees he'd planted in the newly built soil. Their slender trunks and sparse branches were yet too young to be impressive, but the work was evident. Below, alongside the last of the stone steps to the cellar, a young banana tree waved its first huge frond. George's spirits rose, matching his excitement. At least the outside showed labor and care. "About the chickens and rabbits," he said, "I don't like killing them, but when it's a necessity..." He gestured and shrugged silently.

Back in the house, instead of picking up her purse and brief case to leave, Miss Walker sat down at the table again.

George wondered what else would take place. He sat down facing her.

"Have you always taught dance?"

George felt an instant smile on his face. *How did she know I wanted to talk about that?* "No, only the last six years. During the war, I was a toolmaker and production specialist for Westinghouse, in Philadelphia. Even then I did part-time theater. After the war, they asked me to stay on and train for engineering in jet-propulsion turbines, but..." As George shook his head, remembering how much he didn't want to give up theater for engineering, he knew his decision to turn down financial stability must sound weird to a woman like Miss Walker.

He digressed to take the heat off himself. "Lil *always* taught dance, since she was twelve. When I took classes with her and other teachers, I found it to be an extension of acting movement and decided that dance is what I wanted to do."

Even as he said it, he knew it must be gibberish to an agency worker looking for social and economic solidity in a client, but he had to say it. He needed this chance to explain why he'd again taken the unexpected, the unconventional turn-off from the main highway. "Researching many cultures, I found that dance expresses a way of life of a people. I branched out into leading square and folk dancing, and lecturing on folk cultures." He raised both hands in a gesture. "Whatever it takes to make a living. I freelance Square and Folk Dance bookings and teach six classes a week in Modern Dance at the studio."

George looked at Miss Walker to see if he'd lost her miles back. Her eyes hadn't closed. Her hands weren't fidgeting with purse or brief case. "I've explained to Mrs. Keebler that we have extensions in the Mexican, Japanese, Jewish, and Negro areas of LA." George raised his hands in a gesture that accepted his chosen, sporadic way of life and repeated, "Whatever it takes to make a living."

"You made a point of telling Mrs.Keebler that you'd be away six weeks last summer in Mexico. There's a note on your application."

"Yes, we went to see the cultural festivals there. In Mexico City, we studied at the Palace of Fine Arts and brought home some Mexican dances that we taught to our students. We're planning a *Cinco De Mayo* program for next May."

When he stopped talking, George guessed that she was silently questioning how the Liebman couple, making only $6,000 a year, had the money to travel. "Driving our own car," George added, "saved money on transportation and made the trip possible." Then he worried that he and Lil didn't sound stable *if we up and leave when the impulse hits.* "Mrs. Keebler told us there was no chance that a child would be chosen for us over the summer, so we used the time for research."

Miss Walker nodded. "Mr. Liebman, if we go ahead with this..."

"When will we know?"

"I'll need a day or two to sort this out."

George nodded. "Oh."

"If we go ahead with this, I'd like to have an interview with your daughter, Amy."

"Sure."

"Amy alone, just she and I?"

"Yes, that's fine." Miss Walker shouldered her purse strap, took the handle of her briefcase, and stood up. "I'll call you to let you know."

George stood up and nodded. "Fine. Thank you."

"Thank you for your time, Mr. Liebman." She started for the door.

George walked with her and opened it. As she stepped off the porch to the patio, George realized how bumpy the dirt path to the steps was. *A long time before I can cement the patio walk.* "Be careful crossing to the steps, Miss Walker."

"I will."

Silently wishing her safe passage, George watched her until, one hand on the pipe banister, she was on her way down. He went back into the house and closed the door. He stood, not at ease, not comfortable with the familiar items in his own living room, but disoriented, as if, one foot caught in a stirrup, he'd just been dragged by a horse fed on loco weed through the thorny growth of his three lifetimes. Still tumbling through the past, he wanted to collapse in a chair, but instead needed to recheck the interview to know if he, the contrarian, had any chance of being accepted by an establishment agency trying to cookie-cut his dissident life with their conventional regulations. Would they be willing to deliver a baby into his hands? George knew he was asking to be accepted by the establishment, a system of things he'd always found wanting, even corrupt and heartless, which values he'd always opposed. Yet he was subjecting himself to their scrutiny to win their approval. He'd turned over the pot of the many ingredients of his life onto the table. He'd exposed what he'd been, done, succeeded at, failed, achieved, regretted.

With Miss Walker gone, George was left with the spilled ingredients of his life, to look at, to wonder if they'd earned him a passing grade to father a baby. Of course there was no answer yet. Maybe he wouldn't qualify. George shook his head and looked at the clock. Two-thirty. *Only a one-hour interview.* He shook his head again in disbelief. *So much, so much in sixty minutes.*

Chapter 5

The day after Roberta did the Liebman house visit, Jessica was impatient to hear her assessment. She had a hard time keeping her hand off the phone, but restrained herself knowing Roberta needed the morning without interruption.

When Jessica returned from her lunch meeting with the budget committee, her hand went to the phone and buzzed her assistant. "Will it be ready, Roberta?"

"Yes, I'm finishing up."

"Forgive me for being anxious about this, but you understand."

"Of course."

"What does it look like so far?"

"Well, it's a mix; good and bad."

"Oh, dear. Are we making a mistake?"

"We *will* have to consider this carefully. Give me another few minutes and I'll be there."

"All right."

Jessica hung up, dropped back in her chair and rolled her eyes upward. "Oh, God, tell me if I'm doing the right thing." She'd never questioned agency rules before. *This is no way to end a twenty-seven year career. Yet, since the Times wrote that story on our scandalous foster homes, our dirtiest linen is on parade. It's not our secret anymore that taxpayers' dollars are being spent on unacceptable services.* "Roberta, Roberta," she murmured, "I need your support."

Jessica pulled her opened copy of the *Journal of Social Work* toward her, to read for the eleventh time the national statistics on teen pregnancies in America. Again she read their conclusion aloud because she had to hear it to support her contemplated unorthodoxy. "...and California leads the individual states." She slapped the magazine onto her desk and threw up her hands. "*Everyone* knows what we're up against," she muttered. "What am I supposed to do?"

But will Sacramento Steve understand when I tell him I'm bending the rules?

In the sudden silence Jessica backtracked her thoughts. *No, Jessica,* she corrected herself, *don't kid yourself. You're changing the rules. I will have to tell Steve. I can't move this, don't kid yourself. You can't go much farther along without apprising Sacramento.* She was glad for the knock on the door. "Come in, Roberta."

Roberta walked in, handed over her file and sat down beside Jessica's desk, holding herself, as always, prim as a 1908 schoolmarm at afternoon tea.

Jessica opened it immediately and started to read, but closed it as quickly and dropped it on the opened magazine. "I don't want to read the blow-by-blow, Roberta. Tell me, based on your fifteen years of social work experience, is this a possible?"

Roberta pressed her lips together and thought. "Jessica, I don't know." Roberta correctly read the exasperation on her director's face and explained by pointing to the file. "I've only had the one interview with them, with him. His wife had to leave for work."

"You did meet her."

"Yes, she seemed pleasant. On a quick judgement, 'normal'."

Jessica nodded. "Yes, I found them both to be normal and coherent. I would not dare to do this if I didn't think so. But what did you think of him *after* the interview?"

Roberta thought a moment, then raised her shoulders. A slight smile of unease accompanied her words. "I…don't think I've ever interviewed a man…who makes a living teaching dance…tries to make a living. Their combined income is only six thousand a year. *Last* year," she corrected. "This year he said it would be a bit more."

"Six thousand dollars?"

"Yes."

"Is poverty evident?"

"No. The furnishings are simple, make-do." Roberta thought a moment. "They raise chickens and rabbits to supplement their food budget."

"Really." Jessica was remembering the couple sitting in front of her desk. "They look as if they get enough to eat."

"Yes."

"And the house is adequate?"

"A…no, not at the moment. But he showed me the blueprints for two bedrooms, and a foundation. The work is evident. I have a sense that it will get done. They're building a road for direct access to the house."

Jessica looked at Roberta with a small, hopeful smile. "Are we…are we talking a possible?"

Roberta's hands raised slightly as if undecided. "This is not a conventional couple, Jessica. Their work is unusual, and I've checked with their bank. While they have very little, they have never overdrawn their account. Apparently they *can* live within their budget, skimpy as it is. That's in their favor. Not a typical American couple, but there is an honesty…about him that is refreshing. I don't think he's hiding anything."

Jessica sat back, aware that she was subjectively filtering Roberta's statements for her own purposes, expanding the Liebman positives and shrinking the negatives. She smiled as she admitted to herself, *I do want this to work.* Jessica looked at Roberta who seemed to be waiting for the next question. Jessica let her mind race on. *If we decide it's a go, I have no choice but to notify Sacramento. No matter what I think Steve's reaction will be, I have to tell him. He knows teens are sexually active, and our problems with foster homes. Will he see that the Liebmans are providing us with a solution? Not the most exemplary circumstances…* Jessica looked at Roberta. "Are you…in favor of…going ahead with it?"

Roberta frowned. "I…cautiously, Jessica…yes."

Jessica felt a slight gasp…and sat. Roberta had clanged the bell. The starting gate swung open. Yet Jessica sat immobile, silent, faltering. She passed the initiative to Roberta.

"What…what's the next step?"

"Interview the daughter Amy who lives with them."

Jessica nodded…slowly picked up Roberta's file and handed it to her. Jessica smiled weakly. "Let's…let's go ahead."

Chapter 6

Wednesday, Lil drove Amy home from dance class. As soon as they opened the door, George, at the stove mixing the casserole of noodles, ground meat and vegetables, announced, "They're going ahead with it!"

Lil looked at George, not comprehending. Then her tired eyes brightened behind her glasses. "With the adoption?"

"Yes."

"How do you know?"

"Miss Walker called. She wants an appointment with Amy." George grinned at Amy. "She would like to interview you alone."

"Alone?"

"Yes, without Lil or me being there."

"Why?"

"I guess she wants to know how *you* feel about the adoption...about an *inter-racial* adoption, without being pressured..."

"You and Mom didn't pressure me."

"She doesn't know that."

"Yeah." Amy thought about it. "After school?"

"Yes."

"Here? At the house?"

"No. In her office."

"Oh. Choose a day when I'm not dancing."

"Good. If I pick you up at three outside the school, we can make it to her office by three-thirty. Okay?"

"Yes."

"I'll call her. Wash up. Dinner's ready."

George picked up Amy outside her school at three. Driving to the agency, he had no worries about what she would say to Miss Walker. Amy had an ingenuousness that would express the values she'd absorbed in her twelve years. At nine, she performed in an African dance concert with Bob Le House. She'd met and talked with Haitian, Israeli, Mexican, Japanese students and performers who were part of the family's cultural life. Amy's junior high was inter-racial.

Teaching her dance classes, Lil gave the students an hour of technique and devoted a half-hour to the students creating their own movements to express feelings, an idea, a story, or a character. Watching each other's mini-choreographies, the class discussed the pros and cons of the creator's effort. Amy had become skilled in expressing her feelings in a movement capsule. Feelings, *her* feelings, were no strangers to Amy at twelve. George knew she'd have little trouble answering Miss Walker's questions.

Added to Amy's multi-cultural urban life, George recalled the family's work/vacation jaunts to New Mexico. In the summers of '51 and '52, he and Lil worked for the San Cristobal Valley Ranch creating weekly dance and theater activities with guests and Chicano and Indian people of the community. Although the ranch closed after '52, the Liebmans continued to visit ex-ranch owners, Jenny and Craig Vincent and Chicano friends, the Vigils, Trujillos and Martinezes. At the Taos Pueblo, the Liebmans spent time with Pete Bernal and his family. Amy played and rode horses with Pete's granddaughter, Wa-he-la.

George smiled confidently about Amy's coming interview as he checked traffic and moved into the right lane preparing for a turn. *Amy's accepting a child of another race into the house would not be a problem.*

George glanced sideways at Amy to see how she was holding up. He smiled again to recall the conversation at dinner last night, which centered around the pros and cons of having children, and how many. Amy had blurted, "I wanna have ten kids."

As he parked the car, George wondered, *Is this her pendulum swing from being an only child?* Lil and he had repeated that the norm for their financial circumstances would be two children. "You want ten?" George had asked.

"Yes," Amy affirmed.

Walking up the long flight of steps to the agency entrance, George compared twelve-year-old Amy, the young dancer, with that of an eight-month infant they might adopt. *The phrase, 'sibling to Amy,' is not applicable. For a twelve-year old who wants ten kids, 'second mother to the infant' is more appropriate. And Amy could do that well.*

Amy's biological father, Harris, was a lonely man after Lil divorced him. On his bi-weekend visit with Amy, usually an afternoon movie, he'd sit and hold hands with her. At age five, Amy learned that her father needed her emotional support. *At twelve,* thought George smiling, *Amy's already a caretaker. Second mother to an infant will be easy for her.*

Waiting in the lobby while Amy was being interviewed, George skimmed magazine copies of *The Adoptive Parent.* He couldn't connect with pictures of grinning White parents holding their little bundle of White joy toward the camera. *The baby we'll get will not be like us.*

Spread across the middle two pages in large bold print, a headline hooked his attention.

DO YOU TELL THE CHILD HE OR SHE'S ADOPTED?

If the child asks, was the answer in the subsequent long article. The article also hypothesized, 'What if the child *doesn't* ask?' The article was less definitive about that, and seemed to ramble gingerly on, evading finality. *Or is it me?* George asked himself. *Is our special situation getting in the way of my reading this?*

George stopped reading and let the magazine rest on his lap. He looked at the long hallway leading off the far side of the lobby, dotted with many doors to offices. *A White child taken into a White family might never think to ask whether he's adopted.* George tried to picture the different child that he and Lil would get. *A racially-mixed child would be visibly different from us and at some point would ask, "Why am I different?"*

George ran down the family's physical characteristics. Lil is fair with blue eyes. Amy has blue eyes. I have black hair and brown eyes. But indubitably, we all have white skin. The baby? Yet an unknown, but almost guaranteed to be...how dark? How different?

George suddenly realized he was jumping ahead to getting-the-baby stage. *Have we...the house...the plans for two bedrooms qualified?* George looked up again to the long corridor and focused on the door that had closed behind Amy and Miss Walker. He mentally graphed Amy's interview as 'Step B' in the process. *We've gone from 'Step A,' the first interrogation, to 'Step B,' Amy's interview.* George allowed himself to think that the house remodel plans were accepted. *The agency wouldn't waste time if the promise of new bedrooms had not been accepted.*

George felt surprised and pleased at the agency's acceptance of his word that the work would be done. *By contrast,* George gritted his teeth with the annoyance and irritation of it, *the IRS treats us as if we're hiding money from the government and lying about it.* George shook his head angrily. *Garroting people who make six thousand dollars a year!*

Amy and Miss Walker were walking toward him. He closed the magazine, dropped it on the table and went to meet them. A smile lit Amy's face, shone from her eyes. She carried her dancer self as if she'd just finished a performance to thundering applause. George was dying to ask 'How'd it go?' but constrained himself. This was Amy's private occasion to keep as private as she wished.

Miss Walker smiled agreeably and nodded to George, but said nothing.

Amy stood silently, waited for the adults to carry on.

"Thank you for bringing Amy, Mr. Liebman."

George smiled and nodded. "You're welcome." He thought Miss Walker had started to say something more, but stopped. He waited.

She spoke slowly. "I'd like to observe your work at the studio, Mr. Liebman."

"Oh?" *Is Miss Walker ready to take us to step C? Step C, step C, step C* tapped a happy rhythm in his head. "Oh," he said again, feeling the quickening excitement. His voice sounded higher than usual to him. "When would you...?"

"Some day next week?"

"Yes, that would be fine."

"Why don't I call you and we'll set up an appointment."

"Yes, fine." Saying the same thing three times made George feel he was bubbling giddily out of control.

"Goodbye then," Miss Walker said. "'Bye, Amy."

Amy answered, "'Bye."

George was ebullient as they walked toward the doors. "How'd it go, Amy?"

"Fine."

George grinned at himself for asking the wrong question. Probe a teenager who is protecting her new-found power of privacy and expect a non-revealing answer. "Apparently your interview went well."

"Yes."

"You moved us to Step C."

"Step C?"

"The third step in the process. The house, your interview and now she wants to come to the studio."

"Oh."

Amy didn't offer and George didn't press her for excerpts from her interview. It was enough for him that it had moved the adoption to the next level.

That night Lil came home from a dancers' meeting after Amy had gone to sleep. George put the kettle on for tea. He told Lil that Amy's interview seemed to have gone well. "Miss Walker wants to observe my work at the studio."

Lil, about to sit at the table, stopped. "Why yours? Why not mine?"

About to pour the boiled water into the teapot, George halted. "I don't know," he said. "I guess it's the usual prejudice in favor of men."

57

"I'll bet you think you're kidding," Lil snapped.

George looked at her with a wry smile. "No, after hearing your response, I wouldn't dare be kidding."

"I'm the director of *Dance Center."*

George held up his free hand hoping to stall the coming tirade. "True. True."

"Why didn't you tell her to discuss the studio workings with me?"

"I...didn't think of it."

Lil sat herself down, broke a piece of whole wheat toast and spread it with strawberry jam. "That's the trouble. Men take their preeminence for granted."

George moved Lil's mug of hot tea carefully to her plate. "A traditional thinker like Miss Walker automatically thinks of the man as supporting the family..."

"You should have enlightened her."

Toast in one hand, knife in the other, George looked at Lil. "Do you want me to tell her to watch you teach instead of me?"

"When is she coming?"

"I don't know. She said she'd call next week."

"Talk it over with me before you make the appointment."

"OK." George spread jam on his toast. "Miss Walker was impressed with Amy."

"Of course," Lil said. "I knew she would be."

George smiled. "You must be Amy's mother."

Lil started to say something, then stopped.

"What?" George asked.

Lil looked at George, mouth pursed, hesitant.

George read the uncertainty on her face. He stopped chewing and waited.

"Should we ask," Lil began, "for a boy or a girl?"

"Boy," George said in a knee-jerk reaction. He saw the shadow come over Lil's face. "What do *you* want?"

"A girl," Lil said as instantly as George had said boy.

But George didn't hear her response. Before she answered, he was within himself to find out why he'd said 'boy' without even thinking. *My wanting a boy had apparently boiled to the surface long ago and was impatiently waiting to be asked. I want to do it right this time. Do what right? Raise a kid better than I was raised.* His parents fled anti-Semitic Russia and Romania carrying their fears and victim attitudes to America. They burdened their sons with their paranoia. *"In the street, play with Jewish boys only."* Nor did his parents ever talk to him about sex. Orthodox Jews aren't supposed to think about sex until they're married. Automatically, too, first-born son Seymour, was the 'chosen' one, the inheritor of the father's traditions and devotion. Seymour's larger size and strength was ever the painful reminder to George that George was only second best.

Added to George's ignorance of sex, fear of girls, and his painful unimportance to the family, he had to leave Brooklyn College after one semester in 1934 to find work because there was neither food nor money in the house. Kicked into the larger world, he landed on anti-Semitic barbs. All the bank-runner jobs in the *New York Times* classified said, '*Christian only.*'

George did in America what his father did in Russia. Grooming himself with the information about the local *Webster Avenue Presbyterian Church,* he lied to the manager of the employment agency, said he was Christian and got the job. In the second year of his father's apprenticeship as a shoemaker, the '*Christian*' was discovered to be a Jew. His father fled for his life to America. When George's lie was uncovered, Mr. McMasters told George there was no more work at the bank. Added to George's unemployment problems and unpreparedness for dating, he was shamed endlessly by sexual urges that he didn't understand, nor know what to do with. *Is this a way to raise a boy?* About to become a parent again and given the choice, his decision had been made long ago. In raising his son, he would, in part, redo himself.

Realizing he'd sped away from Lil on a different track, he returned and looked at her, realized his ears had heard her say *girl.* Trying to be fair, he wondered, *Should we talk about her wanting a girl?* Tolerance for Lil's wish, however, was dissolved in remembered hot tears during his therapy with Dr. Blumstein. *"Why didn't my parents tell me these things? Didn't they know they were perfecting a shlemiel, a social ignoramus?"*

Still miles away in Blumstein's office, a muddied silence continued between George and Lil. George absently chewed toast and jam and sipped tea. Eventually he remembered that Lil had posed a question, *boy or girl?* George looked at Lil and snapped, "Boy, Lil, I want a boy." Uncomfortable, shamed by unnecessary anger that he couldn't help, George played with his almost empty mug.

Responding to Lil like a Mack truck that had lost its brakes on a downgrade, George spilled another internal load that he'd stacked haphazardly within himself, the fathering of his daughter, Donna. His remorse over his sparse parenting he'd buried under his creative busyness of every day, but it never failed to agitate him. He wasn't seeing her often enough though she also lived in LA. When Donna was five and Amy five-and-a-half, Lil and George thought the two girls would be good playmates for each other. George suggested to Rachel that Donna live with them for a year, as an experiment. The sibling rivalry of the girls for parental affection made that year the worst of George and Lil's marriage. *Whose father is he anyway?* George didn't know how to make Donna feel comfortable in what was clearly Amy's house. Lil couldn't help protecting Amy in the many arguments, as George couldn't help siding with Donna.

Surrounded by three females during that difficult experiment was no help to George who was focused on recreating the boy he should have been. After the year, George returned Donna to Rachel, he, still the guilty, confused father.

Lil had asked, Boy or girl? George's deep compulsions rampaged reason away and tromped on Lil's request. "A boy, Lil," George repeated. "It should be a boy."

Silenced by his repeated blast, Lil looked down at the table, fingered her tea mug, and was quiet.

George won, but felt again the pain of being out of control, of having slammed Lil with his compulsive storm.

Chapter 7

Late Friday afternoon the Liebman phone rang. George and Hank were on separate ladders holding between them the first piece of four-by-eight plywood roof sheeting. Lil and Amy were still at the studio. The phone rang again. "Oh hell, let it ring," George said. They muscled the plywood into place on the new roof joists that replaced *Amy's Alcove*. Still standing on their ladders, they shifted the plywood into place on the joists and Hank hammered the first nail to secure it. The phone rang again.

George hung his hammer in his tool-belt and started back down the ladder. "I'd better answer, Hank. It may be the agency."

"Yeah," Hank said, "I'm all right now. Go ahead."

George scrambled down the ladder and hurried to the phone. It was Miss Walker. "Mr. Liebman, I'm calling about the studio appointment."

"Uh...yes, yes..." George remembered that there was something Lil wanted him to say about the studio appointment. "Miss Walker, did you want to watch my class or Lil's?"

"I was expecting to see yours."

"Would it make any difference?"

"We usually want to know how the husband makes a living."

"Yes." George decided not to drop any roadblocks into the process. "All right, I teach Wednesday, Thursday and Friday. On Wednesday and Friday I conduct a rehearsal after class. We're doing a dance version of *HMS Pinafore*."

"What time do you teach?"

"Three-thirty."

"May I come Wednesday?"

"Sure."

"Thank you. I'll see you then."

61

" 'Bye."

Anxious to get Amy's roof sealed off against winter's heavy nighttime fall of dew, George went out and passed up the next sheet of plywood to Hank. Hank fitted it next to the first one and drove a nail to secure it. "George," he called down, "let's get them all up here, if it's not too hard on you."

"I can do it."

One after another, George slid a sheet off the stack, hefted it to lay against the ends of the roof joists so Hank could pull it up. Hank alternated the plywood sheets, one vertical, one horizontal, so they didn't make one long, vulnerable seam. When all eleven were on the roof, George climbed up to help with the nailing. He alternated his position between squatting and kneeling as he hammered to ease the strain on his knees. He looked over at Hank to see how he was handling it. "You're wearing knee protectors."

"I'd be a cripple by now if I didn't."

With his skilsaw, Hank trimmed the last pieces to fit into the remaining, odd spaces.

George, on his knees, hammered in the last nail. "Done," he said, standing up to stretch out his legs. "Amy won't have to sleep under a tarpaulin." He ran the sleeve of his work shirt across his forehead.

Hank indicated the rolls of tarred roofing paper and bundles of shingles on the ground.

"Wanna lay the tar paper before we quit?"

George looked at his watch. "Oops, no. I gotta make dinner. Tomorrow morning?"

"Yeah. Nine?"

"Fine."

They climbed down. Hank left. George washed up.

Sitting down to eat, George knew he'd have to tell Lil about Miss Walker coming to the studio. "Miss Walker called," he began cautiously.

Lil and Amy stopped eating and waited.

"What did she say?" Amy asked.

George put a piece of mutton in his mouth and turned toward Amy to answer her. "She wants to observe my class."

George felt Lil staring at him before she spoke. "She specifically said *your* class?"

Chewing, George nodded to Lil. "Yes. I asked her if she wanted to observe my class or yours."

"You *did* ask her that?"

"Yes."

"And?"

"She said, quote, 'We usually want to know how the husband makes a living, unquote.'"

Lil stopped eating and boiled silently for a moment. "You didn't say anything else?"

George looked at Lil and shrugged. He spoke quietly. "I thought it best to leave it alone."

Lil exhaled a sudden breath of exasperation and resumed eating.

In the tense silence that followed, George remembered Lil's angry declaration of independence when they were discussing the adoption last year. *"I'm not going to be a housewife stuck at home with a new baby!"* George recalled his response, *"I'll stay home half a week while you teach, and you stay home half a week while I teach."* He remembered how it took Lil by surprise. She couldn't argue with his proposal, but it left her no opening to vent her anger about the abuse of women in our society.

George still felt easy with his last year's offer to Lil. Thinking about it, it was already in place. While Lil was teaching Saturday, Monday and Tuesday, he was working with Hank to get the house ready for the adoption. When the baby came, well, that's how he would spend his time at home, and Lil would still be free to teach all of her classes, and rehearse her young dancers as well. George thought the plan fair and working well. He couldn't understand why Lil was still getting her back up about being subordinated to him.

On Wednesday, George went in to teach his class of nine-year-olds. He alerted Theresa Kennedy, the secretary at the desk in the parent-waiting-room/office, that Miss Walker would be coming to observe his class, and possibly the rehearsal.

Teaching the fifteen children, George forgot about Miss Walker and the adoption until he saw her at the doorway to the studio whispering with Theresa and 'Jack' Jackson, the Negro musical director. Jack stepped aside to let Miss Walker through. Theresa gestured the social worker toward the ramped bench seating of their studio-theater. Miss Walker sat on the front bench as George's children's class began rehearsal of its project for the coming demonstration.

Miss Walker's presence made George aware of the ethnic mix of his eight-to-ten year old class; eleven Caucasians, two Negroes and two Orientals. Pianist Paul Schoop played an eight-bar introduction to *The Whistler and his Dog,* and launched into the carefree melody. One child danced a short solo, then, circling the stage area, she sequentially gathered friends to dance with her. Halfway through, the children stopped moving and stood waiting for teacher's comments and more choreography. The piano trailed off to silence.

"Very good," George said. "You remembered all the movements of the first part well. Before we go on to some new choreography, I'd like you to dance it again. This time, listen to the music. The happy melody should make you feel good."

"Bouncy," one of the children called out.

George smiled. "Yes, bouncy," he agreed. "You're glad to be with your friends. Your movements should be 'feel-good' movements." George looked at their faces, which seemed to be worrying about remembering movements and doing them right. He bent lower to scan the class with a frowning, pseudo-angry face. "Why so grim? You're even allowed to smile when you dance."

Laughter tittered like sudden raindrops.

"Let's do it again. This time let me see you enjoy it."

The second and third times the children danced with more fun and smiles. Then George had them work on new, added movements until the end of the session.

Checking his watch, he gestured to a corner of the studio and called out, "Time for 'over the mountain'."

With bursts of vocal excitement, the children rushed to the indicated corner to line up.

George placed one of his sandals in the center of the studio. "Whose turn is it to lead?"

One of the Oriental girls bounced excitedly up and down, her hand raised. "Mine. Mine."

"Okay. Everyone behind Allison." George demonstrated as he spoke. "Arms are out to the side as you run. You look up and swing up to help lift you in your leap over the mountain."

As George called each child's name, for her preparation run, Paul Schoop made the piano sound like a symphonic drum roll, then exploded a burst of exuberance to lift her for the leap. Each student continued on to the dressing room to change and collect her things.

Meanwhile, teen and adult performers were coming in for the *Pinafore* rehearsal. They seated themselves on the benches behind Miss Walker. Seventeen-year-old Blanca Aguilar, who danced a mood solo in the show, chauffeured the three Echevaria sisters from East LA to rehearse their special trio sequences. George had also cast black-as-a-Masai, Jess Dumas, as *Ralph Rackstraw,* white Evan Hughes as *The Captain* and white Ella Barr, as *Buttercup.*

The children's class over, George came forward in tights and leotard to greet Miss Walker. Still high from teaching he shook hands with her enthusiastically.

Miss Walker dropped her hand quickly and backed off as much as the bench allowed her. George realized that she was uncomfortable with the obvious delineation of his male outlines so close to her. He was reminded again of his unconventional choice; men working for a living don't usually dress in revealing tights.

George stepped back to put her at ease, gestured toward the studio and explained about the class she'd just observed; beside learning how to coordinate their bodies to express their feelings in movement, they were rehearsing a dance for the demonstration that their parents would be invited to. George added, "Please feel free to roam around, ask questions of Theresa in the office or others in the studio."

"Thank you."

The children, now in street clothes, streamed across the studio toward the office where parents were waiting for them. George noticed that Miss Walker's eyes were no longer attentive to him, but darted past to confirm, George guessed, that she was really seeing the color mix of people she was seeing.

Jack went to the piano and warmed up with some musical runs.

"I have to start rehearsal, Miss Walker. You're welcome to stay and watch."

"Thank you." She sat down on the bench.

During the first break in rehearsal, George noticed that Miss Walker was gone. He wondered whether the studio environment had passed the criterion for being granted an inter-racial child, or, her cup of inquiry overflowing with new experiences, Miss Walker had left after seeing all that she could handle, to sip a bit at a time.

The next day George and Lil were returning from their weekly shopping at the downtown LA Public Market. Crossing the dirt path of the patio, they heard the phone ringing. George hurried in, put his shopping bags down and grabbed the phone. It was Mrs. Keebler.

"Mr. Liebman, we've chosen a baby for you."

"Oh? Wonderful!"

Lil came in and in response to her silent question, George held his hand over the mouthpiece and nodded his head vigorously with eyes happily popping. Grinning to Lil, he mouthed a silent *ba-by*. Back on the phone he realized he'd missed something. "I'm sorry, Mrs. Keebler?"

"He's a mix of Chinese and Negro."

"Oh." Whatever George had fantasied, this was a surprise. "Oh," he said again.

"Is…is that all right, Mr. Liebman?"

Any national origin means any national origin. "Yes, yes, that's fine."

"Can you and Mrs. Liebman come in? The first step is to meet him."

"Yes, sure."

"There is nothing binding yet. This first step is to see if there's compatibility, on his part as well as yours."

"Yes."

"Friday morning at ten?"

"No, I teach. Eleven-thirty would be fine. Just a moment, Mrs. Keebler, let me check with Lil." He held his hand over the mouthpiece and spoke to Lil. "Meet the baby, Friday at eleven-thirty?"

Lil thought a moment, then nodded.

"Yes, Mrs. Keebler, that'll be fine."

"Good. We'll see you then."

"Yes. 'Bye."

Lil had sat down at the table to rest. The four stuffed shopping bags were upright on the living room floor. A sudden tumult in his head, George turned to Lil.. He smiled, but was silent. A baby, an all-done-finished-whole baby would be *given* to them. *An unusual mix.*

Going to the sink for a drink of water, George tried to imagine what the baby would look like, but couldn't. *Is such a mix all right?* He turned to Lil. "A Chinese-Negro baby, Lil. What do you think?"

Lil thought a moment, then gestured with one hand as if to say, *"We said, any baby."*

George thought she showed more courage than he. He followed her lead, smiled and nodded acceptance.

Friday morning, George and Lil walked up the many steps of the LA County Bureau of Adoptions. George wondered anew what a Chinese-Negro baby looked like. Since they'd changed their application to read 'any national origin,' it had taken only three months for them to be invited to Step D. George felt silly graphing their progress with the alphabet. They were past the questions of whether or not they were accepted as adoptive parents. *Obviously we've qualified. We're meeting our prospective son! And if we accept the infant, a second visit, with Amy, to meet her intended brother. A Chinese-Negro baby?* George was feeling more stage fright than

67

before a performance. *This is for life!* They walked to Mrs. Keebler's office for orientation.

Chapter 8

The knock on the door bounced Jessica to her feet like a spring. "Come in," she called, aware that her voice was pitched higher than usual. She remained standing to greet the Liebmans and made her smile as welcoming as she could. She even felt that she was fawning. *Can't help it. This couple can make a revolution in California adoptions.* Jessica gestured to the chairs in front of her desk. "Please sit down, Mr. and Mrs. Liebman."

Jessica returned to her chair and reached for their file, which now also included a copy of baby Lee's file. An unsettling thought struck her, slowing her movements. *What if no other White couples feel as the Liebmans do? All these hot-and-cold anxiety sweats for naught?* Jessica dreaded the inevitable hassle with Steve in Sacramento. *Even if he agrees, and that's not certain, if we don't have other White familes asking for a mixed child, we haven't solved anything after all.*

Jessica looked up from the opened file and smiled. *If the Liebmans are bad parents, abusive...even normal people lose their tempers with children. If they don't have enough money and have to go on welfare, I'll be sure to hear about it...if I'm still here when Sacramento hears what I've been up to.*

Jessica's hand trembled as she opened the baby's file in which Emily had included the transfer from the Andersons to the Spinelli's and how he was faring there. Reading from the beginning of the file, she apprised the Liebmans that the infant's mother was an eighteen-year-old Chinese high-school senior who, after giving up her baby for adoption, decided to major in social work. Aware of movement in front of her, Jessica stopped and looked up to see Mr. Liebman smiling, *sarcastically*, she thought. "Mr. Liebman?"

"I find it interesting that becoming pregnant had directed her to social work."

"Yes." Jessica resumed reading. "The father, a Negro in the same graduating class, is a musician. He plays in the school band as well as leads his own combo."

Jessica stopped again to observe the Liebmans' reactions. *They're not fidgeting and looking at the door.* Jessica continued. "During the pregnancy, the parents of the two eighteen-year-olds discussed the possibility of the youngsters marrying and raising the baby. Aside from the burden this would be on their young lives, it was difficult to know where such a couple could live. The Chinese community wouldn't accept a Negro child and vice versa. By common consent the four parents of the students agreed that the baby would be put up for adoption."

Jessica looked at the Liebmans. They were sitting and nodding, not crouching to spring for the door. The husband looked a little bored. *Does he think raising a Negro child outside of Watts will be easy? Both of them are nodding acceptingly as if I'd read them LA's usual weather report; Clear, no change.* Silently, Jessica guessed again. *Probably, they're impatient to see the baby and are not even listening, just being polite to me.*

Jessica felt obligated to help them face some realities ahead. *Whatever it takes to make this adoption succeed.* Jessica put down the file insert she'd been reading from. "The infant, of course, is in a foster home."

They nodded again.

"A third one," Jessica amended. "The first two were...unsatisfactory. We think he's doing better where he is now."

The Liebman's silence continued. Their seeming complacency vexed Jessica. She tightened her lips to restrain her annoyance. *I'm trying to tell them that this child has already run into trouble because of his unusual mix. They're not picking up on it, not asking questions.*

Jessica fingered her pen, handling it into different positions, then tightened it in her fist and pressed her thumb against the top as if testing its strength.

The wife reversed her crossed legs. The husband unfolded his arms, dropped his hands to his lap and tapped his fingers rhythmically against each other. *They don't understand that this is not going to be a usual adoption experience. How do I get them to think about what they may be in for? And not make it seem so tough that I scare them off?*

Jessica loosened her grip on the pen and left it on her blotter. She picked up the final sheet she'd read from, but it offered no further pertinent information about the baby. She put it down. *What...how...to tell them, to prepare them properly? I...we...the agency, we owe them that.*

Aware that she was about to ignore accepted standards of agency-client relationships, before launching herself into the untested air of serendipity, she took in a deep breath and released it. She cautiously entered the verboten world of confidentiality-with-a-client by testing each word before releasing it. "I'm very glad you changed your request on the application."

Her change of pace to an unnatural slowness got their attention. Alert, curious, they waited.

Jessica stopped and nervously worked her lips against each other as if spreading lipstick, though she wore none. She lowered her voice. "You know," she paused to make certain of their complete attention, "these children are considered...unadoptable."

Mr. Liebman's fingers stopped tapping. Mrs. Liebman swung her large purse onto her lap and held it. Jessica continued. "I don't usually say this to clients...This situation is unusual, as you know. I don't usually have the concerns that I have now." *Will they bolt if I tell them all, and three months of anxiety for naught?*

Jessica's voice lowered further, as if she didn't want Steve Gorelni in the Sacramento office to hear. Suddenly words were escaping her like children scattering before a sudden downpour and she was unsuccessfully chasing them to eliminate their panic. "The logjam of mixed children, unadoptable, we're running out of space, overwhelming our resources. We need, despite the law, we need to place them. But it isn't...hasn't been...policy."

Aware that the Liebmans were leaning toward her as she was

71

toward them, Jessica felt that she'd descended to being conspiratorial and stopped again. Their faces were curious, questioning. Jessica sat back and spoke in a more normal voice. "I want you to know that I appreciate the difficulty of raising a Negro child in a White neighborhood. You know…" She stopped again and pretended to look down at the file for further information. The drama of her next thought made her speak as if she were picking her way through an unmapped mine-field, hardly knowing where next to put her foot down.

Because of her returned air of secrecy, the Liebmans leaned forward to hear better.

"Speaking to you, not as director of the agency, but as one who appreciates the nature of your choice, I'd like to be helpful." Jessica doled out her deception word by word. It was not anything she'd planned. It spontaneously fit the needs of her thinking. "You don't have to tell anyone that he's Negro…."

A pair of brown eyes and a pair of blue eyes stared uncomprehendingly at the director.

Jessica looked down again, pretending to read, and continued to space out her offer, word by word. "You could say he's…" she looked up at them, "Korean…." Anxious to know how that falsehood was received, Jessica looked at the man, then the woman. She saw two flashes of silent anger before their faces attempted to return…and not very successfully…to simple interest.

Jessica smiled quickly to assuage any resentment. She spoke softly and rapidly. "I'm thinking of *your* good, Mr. and Mrs. Liebman, and the *child's* good. I mean only to be helpful with this tiny deception. You know how people feel about Negroes. It'll make it easier…I think…perhaps." Her voice trailed off. Hoping to placate their apparent annoyance, her eyes asked theirs, *'Don't you agree?'*

Seeing blank faces, Jessica didn't linger to hear a response, but ran on. "If this adoption works …perhaps …" Suddenly out of breath, Jessica stopped to refuel. She felt impatient to escape from the oppressive friction she'd created.

Curious at her sudden breathlessness, the Liebmans waited.

Jessica headed for the exit. "It's…it's an…in this real world of LA…an option." *Enough!* Jessica thought. *That's as much as I dare say. If they choose to think of their naivete' as courage, that's their choice.*

Focusing herself on the straightening of the file papers and the slow closing of the file, she used this activity to not address them, and spoke without looking at them, "I'll have Miss Walker show you where the visiting booths are." She sat back to remove herself totally from the former confidentiality, lifted the phone but held it without dialing. She looked at the couple and spoke to them in a tone that said, 'This is the voice of the State of California speaking through me, the director of this agency.' "We are *very* anxious for this adoption to work, Mr. and Mrs. Liebman, more than any other."

Jolted by the director's abrupt change from confidentiality to formalism, the Liebmans glossed over their negative feelings about her offer, and, anxious to move it along, nodded to tell her they carried no resentments for her deviousness.

Jessica wanted more specific, expressed confirmation from them to her last statement. She looked at the husband, then at the wife. They didn't seem to catch on. She thought to spell it out. "This…this adoption is a…first." She again looked from one to the other, the phone in her hand remained poised. Still uncertain, before opening the agency's gate for them to enter the road from which there was rarely any turning back, she wanted them to tell her that they understood how significant this event was. "A first of its kind," she added.

Seeing that she was waiting for something from them, George said, "…Yes, yes, of course," and added, "We're anxious too, that it work."

Jessica looked at Mrs. Liebman.

Mrs. Liebman nodded. "Of course."

Jessica dialed. "The Liebmans are here, Roberta." She hung up. As if the Liebmans had already been dismissed and left the office, Jessica ignored them while she opened the active file drawer and made much of putting the closed file into its alphabetically correct place. Roberta knocked. "Come in."

The Liebmans stood up.

Immediately after the greetings, Miss Walker said to the Liebmans, "Please come with me."

Away, finally, from the authoritative dominance of Mrs. Keebler, George and Lil were relieved to be in the quiet, restrained presence of Miss Walker. Accompanying her, George pursued thoughts he hadn't permitted himself in Mrs. Keebler's office. *Anxious? She's anxious about this? Lil and I are the ones who have to make it work. Is she asking us to sign a guarantee that we'll solve all his problems and turn out an extraordinary adult?*

Walking slowly with Miss Walker through the office area to the lobby, George continued to silently juggle the hot coals Mrs. Keebler had thrown to them. *Unadoptable? Meaning no family, White or Negro, wants him?* The laughing, bouncing exuberance of the children in his classes erased any questions concerning their ethnicity. *They're children.* George used rhythm, melody and dance action to dissolve the inner obstacles blocking each child's flow of expression. *Unadoptable?* George shook his head. *Children are children.* The agency's archaic policy seemed more archaic, the director's unexpected dishonesty offering them the opportunity to hide the baby's heritage seemed more pathetic, in light of George's present and past activities.

As shop steward during war production at Westinghouse, he upgraded qualified Negroes from sweepers to machine operators. Those many incidents and the ease of his New Mexico friendships with Chicanos, Indians and all ranch guests virtually eliminated the race ingredient in his dealing with people. *And Keebler suggests we hide the baby's identity? Keep the child's identity secret from himself?*

Before this orientation interview George had felt that he'd advanced beyond the agency's outdated racial policy and had pitied parents who couldn't love a child across the racial barrier. Through the agency's interviews he'd been able to keep silent about his opinions. When Mrs. Keebler dropped the Korean bomb on them, George was hard put to restrain his anger. Exploding in opposition to her proposal, however, could have prejudiced the director's opinion about the Liebmans being appropriate adoptive parents. *Lil and I are wanting a child, in caps. All our lives we've walked gingerly to avoid land mines that ignorance and greed of others buried in our paths. We've learned to pick our way as carefully as Keebler seems to be doing, for whatever her reasons.*

George remembered feeling the same anger during the war, the day he walked into the quarter-mile long Westinghouse plant newly built to help defeat Hitler...

It was 'festooned' with anti-Semitic leaflets on every one of its 162 machines, so unexpectedly visible as to look like snow had fallen inside the plant. Picking one up and reading it, George fumed and dashed upstairs to complain to Westmaas, the personnel director. George barged into his office and thrust the leaflet under Westmaas' bulbous Dutch nose, almost forcing his blue eyes to cross trying to look at it. "Read this!" George commanded. It was a long poem about the clever Jew who got tires for his car when the Irishman, the Italian and the 'other Americans' couldn't get them under the war rationing.

Westmaas read it and grinned. "It's funny."

George blew. He grabbed the leaflet from Westmaas' hand and again pushed it toward his nose. His fury drove him close to Westmaas' face. "Don't you realize what this means?"

Westmaas leaned back.

"What this means in battle?" George pressed him. "Why should a Jew help a wounded buddy who tells anti-Semitic jokes?" George shook the leaflet in Westmaas' face. "This *divides* them! *Destroys* teamwork! We need the army to work together!" George pointed to the clean type of the flyer. "Look at the printing. This is not some two-bit job. This was done on a Westinghouse press!"

"Okay, okay, George." With a shaking hand, Westmaas took the leaflet from George. "I'll...I'll take care of it."...

Still feeling the fury of dealing with Westmaas, following behind Miss Walker, George felt he was again out front, all alone. He reached for Lil's hand.

Surprised, Lil looked at him. George and Lil were never touchy-feely in public, but this was one time George needed to know that at least Lil was with him. He held her hand as they walked.

Seeing the slim back of Miss Walker's pale blue suit and the touch of Lil's hand brought George back to the present. It caused him to think about what the adoption meant. *I've never done this before. Despite inter-racial activities, I've never lived with any but Caucasians. My activism was one underdog's effort to protect others from our complex, often cruel, system. I didn't take one of them home, however, to live with me.*

George realized that adopting the inter-racial baby was not just arguing for the baby's right to live a good life. *Can I live equitably with one of another race? Can I love and be father to this different child? Will he want too be my son when he discovers he's different from me?*

Self-doubts were tumbling in George's head when Miss Walker stopped and turned to the Liebmans. They were in an alcove part of the lobby removed from the walk-through and waiting areas. They stood near a line of five booths upholstered in black leather, that might have been donated by some up-scale restaurant, but without the table. Each booth of two, facing semi-circular seats enclosed a six-foot space. The high backs provided privacy from those in adjacent booths.

George and Lil stood waiting for further instruction, unprepared for and puzzled by Miss Walker's next actions. She looked around to assure herself that they were the only ones in the interview area. They were, but she lowered her quiet, restrained professional voice yet more, to almost a whisper. "You know, Mr. and Mrs. Liebman, we on staff have talked about this… experimental…adoption a great deal."

George and Lil leaned toward her to hear better.

"We want to make it as easy for you as we can."

Miss Walker's sudden, unprofessional descent to a confidential tone surprised the Liebmans. Recalling Mrs. Keebler's hushed voice,

George felt that he and Lil were being surreptitiously passed from one spy operative to another in some secret plot.

"We thought," Miss Walker continued, but so uncomfortable in this strange role, she fumbled with broken, hesitant phrases, "that...if you want...you don't have to tell anyone...or the baby...that he's a...Negro."

George clamped his mouth shut to avoid an anger explosion.

"You could say," Miss Walker went on with a tiny, self-satisfied smile, as if offering them the perfect solution, "that he's Korean."

Before the stunned silence got embarrassing, George said, "Yes," but endangered himself for an ulcer by swallowing the bitter sarcasm that boiled in his mind, *and thank you for favoring us fellow Whites with this good ol' boy option.* "Yes," he repeated through tight lips, "Mrs. Keebler mentioned it."

Miss Walker nodded, satisfied that she'd proved her agency support by repeating the under-the-table offer.

Having served the contraband bonbon for their taken-for-granted racist sweet-tooth, Miss Walker stepped back to create again the proper space between herself and her clients. She explained the sequence of the first visit. "Miss Emily Karelin, the baby's social worker, will bring him here in a few minutes. She and the baby will sit with you in the booth." Miss Walker stopped abruptly. Her face darkened. She turned and left, leaving George and Lil waiting. They looked at each other, wondered whether they should sit in the booth or wait standing.

Interrupting them, a surprisingly young-looking, brown-skinned Miss Karelin, cradling an infant swathed in white in her arms, approached the Liebmans. She gently jiggled a blue rattle for the baby's attention and talked softly to him. Behind her, George saw Miss Walker hovering at the far wall of the lobby, watching, that disturbed look still on her face.

The long-awaited baby's presence set off anxiety waves in George. Realizing his tensions were bringing him close to tears, he attempted to calm himself by breathing more deeply and slowly.

Miss Karelin stood before the booth with them, smiling and

nodding hello. Her hair was cropped close to follow the shape of her head, fitting like a hat of small curls. "It's better if you sit down," she said with a gentle smile.

George walked into the booth followed by Lil. They were surprised by the sudden feeling of privacy it created. Miss Karelin lowered herself next to Lil. She cooed soothingly to the infant, rocked him gently in a slow rhythm.

Out of the baby's darkish skin, the Oriental eyes seemed strained by fear. They looked first at Lil, then at George. The nose flared at the nostrils, broad for the thin face. Moisture collected the down of fine hairs on his head, sweating them into black threads stuck to his scalp.

"He knows there's going to be a change," Miss Karelin interpreted.

'Any national origin' had been an easy phrase to write on paper, but the thought that this child would be thrust into his arms, into his house to raise…? George's mind raced ahead to explore the challenge of it. *"This is my son,"* I'll be saying to the registrar at his school. *"This is my son,"* I'll be saying to colleagues. This unique face and body will be mine to rear, to mold…

George reached across Lil to touch the infant's tightened fist. The baby's eyes wrinkled shut as the toothless mouth opened and yowled a protest.

Miss Karelin gave the rattle to Lil and raised the baby to her shoulder, patted and stroked his back. "There, there, Lee," she soothed, "it's all right. These are good people."

When the baby quieted, Lil asked if she could hold him.

Miss Karelin looked at Lee resting in her arm, silent now, but staring apprehensively. She reached the baby toward Lil.

The movement caused the baby's face to pucker.

Lil smiled and raised the rattle for the baby to see, but the pucker deepened.

"Maybe we'd better wait a bit," Miss Karelin said.

Miss Karelin's sensitivity as the baby's advocate impressed George. He and Lil settled back in their seats, to look and smile, to silently tell the baby they were friendly. "Is Lee his name?" George asked.

"No. The first foster mother called him that because he's Chinese. We use it only as a label to identify him when we discuss his case. You can give him any name you'd like."

Lil raised the rattle again to attract the infant's gaze. The baby saw it, but didn't reach for it. Lil handed the rattle to George and lifted both hands toward the baby.

His stare seemed to go from fearful to curious.

Lil's hands went closer, then touched the receiving blanket on either side. She made as if to lift him.

The baby's head made weak little movements to each side as if trying to see what was caused him to be touched.

Lil grinned as she lifted him to her.

George shook the rattle softly toward the baby hoping to distract him from his fear.

He went to Lil, tense but silent.

George grinned to him and offered the softly shaking rattle.

The baby's face puckered.

Too much, too soon, George decided. He sat back, removing himself from the baby's attention.

Lil continued trying to soothe him, but he was convulsively working up to a yowl. Lil handed him back to Miss Karelin.

George felt they were dead-ended.

Perhaps in agreement, Miss Karelin smiled and nodded as if to say 'It has gone well,' but she said nothing. George noted her competent, low-key handling of Lil and himself. *Especially in this case, a first...an experimental first for the agency. Staff seems to be trained to not influence the adopting parents' decision.*

George doubted that Miss Karelin had been let in on the decision to offer the Korean option. Negro herself, she would be angered at their proposal to hide his identity. Probably only the top echelons were trusted to handle that barrel of gunpowder.

George and Lil walked out of the agency, slowly, thoughtfully. George felt overwhelmed. He thought he'd had much contact with non-Caucasians, yet imagining his living with a child who looked so different, being responsible for his daily activities, his healthy growth…it felt awkward and apart from his life. *Or is it that any addition to the family would be a dislocation? Look what happened when we tried to incorporate Donna into our daily lives. If Lil had been able to have our own baby, would a natural birth been just as disruptive?* Imagining a baby in the house; all the interruptions, sleepless nights and illness unknowns, it was obvious. *Of course, All change is awkward. The trick is to figure out how to handle it.*

Outside in the sunshine, going down the long ramp of steps, George and Lil were still silent. George wondered if he was wrestling with some prejudice hidden from his consciousness until now. Anger at the remembered agency's offer to deny the baby his race, fried George's brain, fogging his ability to think. He shook his head at the unexpected complexities. However, he didn't let himself off the hook by blaming Mrs. Keebler for his turbulence. *Why do I feel awkward at the thought of running the daily life of this infant? My past activities for equal rights, to implement them regardless of race, creed or color, were perhaps not as deeply felt as I thought.*

George looked at Lil as they continued down the stairs. *What's Lil thinking? Is this shaking her up as well?* He glanced at her again. Her face seemed as tumultuous as his feelings. Yet *our silence seems to take for granted that this baby will be our son. Really?*

Have we accepted that? This first visit was only a test. George remembered that the process would continue with Amy accompanying them on a second visit, as if there would be no other thought than that the baby would be theirs. *Is he what we want? Are there options? Can I say to this infant, "I've seen your brown skin, Oriental eyes, and broad nose and I'm going to hold out for a prettier baby"? No, prettier has nothing to do with it; one more familiar, more like me.*

What's 'prettier' anyway? Anglo-Saxon pretty? Blond hair, blue eyes? They're the ones who discriminated against me because I'm black-haired, brown-eyed and Jewish. George felt the heat of the sun making him sweat. *Race is no basis for judging a person. Yet it's served up every morning in America with bacon and eggs, causing us national indigestion.*

George was beginning to feel some satisfaction, some peace that he genuinely believed race had nothing to do with it, when the word, *unadoptable,* set off a delayed explosion in his head. *Unadoptable? By whose standards? This baby's not entitled to enjoy what's automatically granted to Caucasians because of different physical features? Not as American as those with white skin?*

As they reached the last step George learned that his heart was where his words were, but it did not bring him the peace he expected. The agency's need for duplicity meant that the hatred of 'others,' those outside the blonde-hair-blue-eyed circuit, is no less embedded in American life now than it was, even among those who proclaim to practice otherwise. Even fighting the war against Fascism, Negroes were segregated. Is it endemic in the country? George shook his head. *What peace?* This recurrent awareness of racism kicked him in the gut again, sickened him. *We 'others' are still not safe in America.*

Chapter 9

Jessica reached for the phone, picked it up...put it down. Undecided, her hand remained on it. *How will Steve react? He knows the plight of the kids...spoken up for them hundreds of times when he was with LA Child Care, but he got kicked up to administration; budgets, political compromises.* Jessica remembered Steve's new refrain; "I have a legislature to deal with, Jessica. *We have to do the politic thing.* Jessica summed up the new Steve; *by-the-book is his bible.*

She left the phone in its cradle and sat back in her chair. I'll talk to Roberta first. Make certain the Liebmans are a possible. They've had their first visit with the baby. Poor Lee, thin and frightened, not the Shirley Temple of babies. Thinking of other possible outcomes for this experiment, Jessica shrugged, acknowledged that all the factors were still fluid. *Maybe the Liebmans are not so sure they want a child of 'any national origin'. They might turn Lee down. It's too soon to talk to Steve.*

Relieved that she'd worked up an excuse for not calling Steve, Jessica turned away from the phone, but then felt guilty about being afraid to divulge her secret to her supervisor. She rationalized. *If the Liebmans don't accept Lee, there's nothing imminent. It's just as well I don't rush to tell Steve what I'm thinking.* She fidgeted, pulled the Liebman file, fingered the edges, but didn't open it, put it away. Feeling her future with the agency at stake, she thought of possibly introducing the revolution gradually. *Maybe I should send a letter to Steve suggesting the idea, ask his opinion.* Thinking about it, that seemed a safe way to go, more like the way an agency director with a vision would handle it. *But I need to talk to Roberta. Why? Ask her if she thinks it's the right time to let Steve in on it?*

Feeling her rising tension, Jessica became aware that she'd moved this case beyond what could be considered a director's courage to test the waters of a new policy. Hostile Health and Welfare Committee legislators could gleefully accuse her of pursuing an illegal course and fire her. The thought of being fired sent her insecurities rocketing. *Is it worth the blood pressure?* Jessica shook her head. *This is too big for me to carry alone.* She picked up the phone and rang Roberta.

"Roberta, can I bounce something off you?"

"Of course."

"Come in for a minute."

"I'm just leaving for an interview with the Wheelers."

"Oh." Jessica remembered Roberta's woodenness in the embrace. *Maybe she's afraid of another.* "I'll tell you now, Roberta."

"Yes."

Jessica carefully scanned what to say. *Even if Nancy listens in on the switchboard, it won't give anything away.* "I'm thinking of calling Steve and apprising him.

"Oh?"

"What do you think? Is it too soon?"

During the silence, knowing Roberta's cautions about functioning outside of parameters, Jessica was patient. She imagined Roberta's pursed lips tightening.

"No-o..." sounded Roberta's careful opinion. "It might even be helpful...to prepare him..."

Encouraged by Roberta's voting with her, Jessica waited to hear more. Nothing further, however, so Jessica offered an affirming "Mm-mmm."

"I think," Roberta continued slowly, "if he objects, refuses to consider it, it'll be our signal to stop the process here and not spend any more time and energy on the Liebmans."

"Yes." Silence again. *What more?* Jessica questioned herself. The continuing silence meant both agreed all options were covered. *What else am I waiting for? Do I want her to come and hold my hand?*

"Yes," Jessica repeated. "Thanks, Roberta."

"You're welcome."

"Check back with me," Jessica added hurriedly.

"I will."

The line clicked. Jessica cradled the phone slowly, let her hand slip off and sat back in her chair. *No excuse, Jessica, for further delay.* Jessica took a deep breath. *Blood pressure, stay down, and that's an order!* Jessica closed her eyes and exhaled with a noisy flutter of her lips. She breathed in deeply and exhaled again, then reached forward and picked up the phone. "Nancy, get me Steve Gorelni at the Sacramento office." Jessica hung up and waited. Checked her nails, *No, too soon to have them done.* She opened the drawer marked 'Active,' but knew she couldn't focus and closed it again. The ringing phone startled her. "Yes, Nancy."

"He's out of his office. I left a message for him to call you."

"Do you know when he'll return?"

"His secretary said the meeting could take one or two hours."

"Thanks, Nancy." Jessica hung up, bounced out of her chair and walked to the restroom.

Steve called right after lunch with an exuberant, "Hi, Jessica." His voice sounded like he was genuinely glad to talk to her again. *Encouraging,* thought Jessica. She recalled his complimentary remarks about her twenty-eight years of devotion to the children, when he was still on staff. *Maybe, maybe he'll be on my side in this one.* "I...I'm in the middle of making a decision, Steve. I was informed by County General to expect another crop of mixed babies. I already have eighty-one in foster homes and only two Negro possibles asking, and you know about the *Times* expose' on foster homes."

"Yes."

"Six months since the exposé, the foster care crisis is no better."

"Yes, I know."

With all that he's handling in Sacramento, Jessica wondered how much attention he could pay to her local problems. *But he must be hearing about this happening in other cities.* "Steve," she started again, "a White family asked for a mixed baby."

Silence. Jessica heard a soft crackle of static on the line, then silence again. She knew he was rerunning her tape, digesting it. "A

White family asked for a mixed baby?"

"Yes, quote, a baby of any national origin, unquote."

"They said that?"

"Their very words."

"And?"

Jessica took a deep breath and let it out. "I'm...processing... them."

"You are?"

"Yes."

"Why?"

"Because, Steve, I'm...the agency...the county...is desperate."

After another silence, Steve spoke slowly. "Jessica, you're climbing a ten-foot wall and nothing to grab onto."

"Yes, there *is*, Steve, the plight of these infants, the precious, precious year from zero to one. We're responsible for eight of those twelve months..."

"Jessica," Steve interrupted, "I'm aware of how difficult it's getting. I have all the stats on teen pregnancies here in my office. But you're asking me to lead the charge to change the politics in California."

"If not you, Steve, who?"

"Flattering, Jessica, but it could be suicide."

In the silence, Jessica wondered where the conversation would go. *Where can it go?* she asked herself.

"I've only been here a year, Jessica," Steve said slowly, as if to make sure she would not misunderstand him. "My family likes it here. I like being kicked upstairs. Suicide is not a priority."

"Asking for the eight-hour day was once thought of as economic heresy."

"Jessica, progress in Los Angeles and San Francisco does not translate easily to rural California."

"Steve, there must be enough decency out there to save these children."

"There are also conservatives and racists who believe fiercely in segregation and who sponsor politicians to make their laws."

"I know it's not easy, Steve, but you could talk to the Health and Welfare Committee and see if it's got a breath of a chance."

"Are you adding it to my agenda?"

Jessica hesitated. "...Only, if you agree."

"Of course I agree..."

"You do?" Jessica wondered if he said that to tell her he's still the same guy at heart about kids. *Will he say that to politicians?*

"Jessica," Steve snapped, "I can't accomplish all that I...you and I believe in. Politics doesn't work that way."

"But it could mean releasing these children to permanent placement. Isn't that what we're here for? And we'll cut down a huge foster home expense." Jessica couldn't resist the sarcastic, "Wouldn't the politicians like that. They hate spending money on children."

"Not all of them, Jessica. Fortunately, not all."

Because of Steve's mixed response, in the silence that followed, Jessica encouraged herself by imagining she heard his wheels turning. *Is he trying to find a way? Good enough. He knows what I'm talking about. He has the stats.*

"Jessica, do you have that many families lined up?"

Jessica's heart sank. Steve went right to the basics and she wasn't prepared. "No, but if you give me the go-ahead, I'll do a PR campaign..."

"It's not up to *me*, Jessica, to give you the go-ahead. I don't make or change the laws of California. You've got to understand that!"

"I do, Steve, I do." But he'd given Jessica enough moral support for her to wonder what next...*how* next? Jessica lowered her voice to a quiet, timid. "Shall... shall I continue to process this family?"

"Yes. I'll talk to my policy staff and get back to you, Jessica." The line clicked.

Jessica slowly cradled the phone and hung on it as she hung on to Steve's little word, *Yes. At least I can tell Roberta to keep the process going.* Jessica sat back, put two fingers on her wrist pulse, closed her eyes and breathed deeply.

Chapter 10

Amy rode with her parents for the second visit. Lil drove with George beside her, Amy in back. Wondering what kind of anxieties Amy might be having, George turned to ask how she was doing. Her cheek was propped on her fist against the window, watching traffic slide past, her full lips pushed forward. Though looking out, her thoughts seemed deeply inward. George turned front. *Figures*, he thought. *Two months ago, Lil told me Amy started to menstruate. Big change. Getting a baby brother, big change in the family. Big changes for Amy, inside and out. How well will she handle them?* George recalled Amy during yesterday's dance rehearsal of the *Young Dancers* in the studio. Lil showed the group a new choreography to Prokofief's *Winter Holiday* suite. The young dancers watched Lil demonstrate the movements and Amy was the first to repeat the phrase accurately.

George smiled. Amy's been watching dance classes since she was one-and-a-half. Moving to music was as much her language as 'mama' and 'da-da.' But this physical growing up, hitting puberty...George shook his head. As frightening as puberty was for him, George knew it was more so for a girl. Amy was a good student. George wondered whether it would affect her grades. *At twelve, she has her school routines under control, gets good report cards. All of a sudden she's thinking things she didn't worry about before, wondering what it would be like to step out onto the boyfriend road the girls are always talking about. Then she listens to Lil explain how to keep herself sanitary, presentable, and not be embarrassed. And from then on, it's something new with her body every day.*

Long past the worst of it himself, George smiled wistfully at the confusion physical growing up had meant for him; his ignorance and the painful taunts of boys who didn't believe he didn't know and didn't do what they had so gleefully discovered. Ignorance and fear had delayed the usual stages for him.

Also new for Amy; after twelve years of being the only child, she'll have a baby brother, hers to partly care for. Is she still enthusiastic about the adoption? And about having ten kids of her own?

Inside the agency Amy and Lil went to the meeting booth while George told Nancy at the switchboard they had arrived for their appointment.

Miss Walker didn't show this time. In a few minutes, Miss Karelin, cooing and trying to focus the baby on the blue rattle, was crossing the lobby toward them. She greeted the Liebmans and sat beside Lil. Amy and George watched Lil, taking her cue from Miss Karelin, cooing to get the baby's attention.

This time, twelve days since the first visit, George looked at the baby through Amy's eyes. His face was still very thin, his color sallow. George looked at Amy to see her reaction.

Her smile had faded. She frowned, then smiled attentively to the baby.

Lee was clearly unused to so many people. Alert, fearful, with sudden movements of his head, he looked at each of them, then back to Lil, the closest. He puckered, but then changed his mind about crying.

Lil reached toward him. "May I hold him?"

Miss Karelin shifted her position and in slow motion lifted the baby to Lil.

Lil cradled him, talked quietly, soothingly.

He seemed to accept it.

Miss Karelin offered the rattle to Amy.

Amy took it, leaned toward the baby and shook it gently. "Hi there. Hi."

Lil was trying to hum. George admired her courage. He and Lil were Johnny-one-noters. George extended his arms. "May I hold him, Lil?"

Lil turned, lifted him across Amy and gave him to George.

George brought his arms close, cradling the infant. "Hi there, fella." George grinned to him.

The baby's look continued somber, inquiring.

"He's doing better this time," Miss Karelin said.

"Yes," Lil agreed.

"Can I hold him, Pops?" Amy asked.

"Sure." George lifted him to her.

Just as the baby arrived in Amy's arms, he voiced his first complaint of the session.

Amy cradled him and sang, *"Hush little baby, don't say a word..."* Amy's voice was musical. The sounds of the first line surprised the baby out of his crying. Amy rocked him easy with the lilt of the music as she continued,

> *Mama's gonna buy you a mockingbird.*
> *If that mockingbird don't sing*
> *Mama's gonna buy you a diamond ring.*

By the fourth line, however, the baby was squirming, turning his head to look, apparently for Miss Karelin.

She reached and took him. "Well, you had a good visit this time, Lee."

George was jarred again by the baby's pseudo-name, but in the preparation for the good-byes didn't think about it further.

The visit over, they took turns leaning toward the baby and saying, "Goodbye, Lee."

Miss Karelin lifted the baby's little hand and waved it to each of them. She stood up with the baby and addressed the Liebmans. "Miss Walker will call you in a few days."

Smiles, nods and thank yous were said all around. Miss Karelin started back across the lobby with the baby.

The Liebmans were silent as they walked slowly toward the doors. George was anxious about Amy's reaction. "What do you think, Amy?"

"He looks undernourished."

"You think so?"

"His face is so thin. And his color is poor."

"It seems unusual, but I thought it was due to his ethnic mix."

"No, there are kids at school who are mixed. They have a healthy color. It's different."

George thought about that, which led him to Miss Karelin's statement when she first showed the baby to George and Lil. She'd explained the baby's fearfulness with, *He knows there's going to be a change. Change? Mrs. Keebler said he'd been taken out of one foster... no, two foster homes to a third. The poor kid hasn't had anything but change.*

George repeated his thoughts to Amy and Lil. "He's already been through a lot of changes." They opened the heavy glass doors and stepped into the sunshine. "But when we take him home," George continued, as they started down the steps, "and give him lots of love and nourishment, he'll look better, and he'll stay in one place for a long time."

Lil and Amy seemed to silently agree. None questioned the agency's policy of keeping the baby for his first eight months to complete the legal level of required testing before releasing the infant to the adoptive parents. The Liebmans seemed to think that was small potatoes against having him to raise and influence for all of his life.

Chapter 11

Jessica had a disturbing, dream-filled, night. She saw her late husband, Leonard, slowly unwind from his throes of contorted pain to stretch out on his back and lie quietly, relaxed once again to his full length. He even had a small smile on his face. *At last,* thought Jessica in her dream, grateful that the morphine was working, *he's at peace.* Suddenly she heard her son Jonathan calling to her. She saw him, far in the distance on a finger of land thrust into the sea. Swinging his arms, he looked like a wind-up toy. He swung an arm forward, as if throwing something to her. Suddenly a ball of cord came toward her. Unwinding, it became smaller and smaller as it came closer, until only the end of it reached her. She caught it and called back to him, "I've got it, Jonno, I've got it." Jessica pulled on it, thinking to draw Jonathan back to her, but he stood where he was, legs braced against rocks and holding his end of the cord with both hands. To keep from being pulled off balance, Jessica also leaned back, dug in her heels and held on with both hands.

On Jessica's left, Hulda was running toward the stretched line as if racing to be first to the tape. "No, Hulda, no," Jessica called out, "don't break the cord."

When Hulda grabbed the rope with both hands, the momentum of her run lifted her legs into a giant swing that Jessica remembered seeing and admiring teen-age Olympic gymnasts perform. "Hulda! Hulda!" Jessica called out, "you can't do that!"

But Hulda was doing it. Her body stretched to a long line from hand to toes, and swung a perfect circle. As she started up again, she let go and momentum lofted her onto a cloud above her, where she sat laughing and waving as she sailed away.

More pattering steps on Jessica's left were runners Grace, Alicia and Janice, one behind the other, heading for the cord. Above each sailed a cloud for them to land on.

"Where's Emily?" Jessica shouted to them. "Where's Emily?"

But they were too intent on executing their giant swings to answer. Grace was the first to grab the rope.

"No! No!" Jessica called. "You can't do that!"

But Grace swung, let go and landed on her cloud.

Jessica frantically asked the remaining two, "Where's Emily?"

But Alicia and Janice weren't listening. Alicia swung with Janice right behind. They landed on their clouds and were gone.

Jessica heard heavy footsteps to her left.

Emily came running more slowly, holding the baby Lee against her body.

"No, Emily, no," shouted Jessica, "you'll drop him."

Emily shifted Lee to a one-hand hold and grabbed the cord with the other. She swung herself into the beginning of the giant swing…

In mortal terror, Jessica bolted upright shouting, "No, Emily, the baby!" Her heart was pounding. She was drenched in sweat. Realizing it was a dream, she fell back on her pillow and added tears of relief to her distress. Despite her sobs, she attempted to normalize her breathing by sucking in draughts of air to lower her pressure, which she knew must have peaked.

Having had Jonathan home for a week before she took him and Jimmy to the LA airport, had made her newly aware of his presence in the house. "Oh," she muttered in relief, "I'm so glad he's not here. He would've thought I'd gone mad." She shook her head in wonder at what she'd been through in the last minutes. "Talk about taking your work home," she muttered with an ironic smile.

Her bedroom was dark. It was a clouded autumn night and no moonlight filtered into the house. She pulled the chain of the small lamp on her nightstand to read the clock. "Only twelve-thirty. Good. I can still get a night's sleep." She turned off the lamp, lay down on her side and drew her knees up.

But she hadn't received this week's note from Jonathan as he'd promised. When driving the two of them to the airport, she'd insisted, "Not a card, Jonathan, a note in an envelope, *air mail.* If you write cards, you'll arrive home before they will."

From the back seat, where the boys were sitting, Jonathan leaned forward to argue with her. "So the airplane goes down and my letter doesn't arrive. What're you gonna do? Call some international missing persons bureau? Mom, we can take care of ourselves. We'll be fine."

"All right, all right, Jonathan, write the letters anyway. Keep your part of our agreement."

Jonathan slid back in his seat. "Yeah, Mom, I will."

But when Jessica settled down to sleep again, it had been ten days since she'd had word from her son. Jonathan had surprised her by writing three lengthy letters from *Kibbutz Revi* in Israel, where both boys were allowed to stay temporarily in exchange for work. The two young Americans discovered that, busy with building a cooperative life in their new homeland, the *kibbutzniks* rarely talked about religion, except to castigate the Orthodox Jews who wanted the government to use the Bible as its guide rather than the western, democratic format, which had been verbally agreed on by all political parties. Jonathan wrote that the people on *Kibbutz Revi* focused on providing a home on their Kibbutz for Jewish refugees, making the land productive and building their collective's economy.

As one of the 'left' cooperatives, *Revi* focused intensely on these goals. Living and working together and sharing common goals they created new social experiments. Jessica was delighted that Jonathan wrote at length about the things he was discovering. *Jonno may not like Poly-Sci in America,* Jessica mused, *but he certainly seems to be enjoying it abroad.* She was ready to admit that, despite her objections to his leaving school, traveling seemed to have reinvigorated his interest in learning. In her dream she replayed a vacation she and Lenny took to visit the social experiments in Israel…

In the late thirties, when she and Lenny were young in the social-work field, they had shouting discussions with fellow staff workers about the social experiments that some collectives were attempting. "What can be wrong," Lenny had argued, "with giving men and women and their children a family home in exchange for their work for the community?" Members of the collective were given free medical care, and a minimum amount of money for personal shopping in the city. The communal kitchen and nursery freed the parents to work.

To American conservatives, who hated the rise of the Soviet Union as the great threat to US Capitalism, the collective living experiments in Israel were too close to Russia's efforts to build a Communist society. "Collectivism will break down American Free Enterprise!" The campaign of reaction was largely successful. A phobic fear in America spread like a thick ooze that was deadening creative thought. Experimental thinking was quickly dubbed, 'Communistic' and conservatives spat the word 'liberal' with venom. Jessica's dream flared again with the shouting arguments she and Lenny had with their fellow social workers. Jessica and Lenny thought it brave and bold of the Israeli collectives to experiment with common bathrooms and showers for boys and girls through their teen years. "Would it make for better marriages," wondered the Keeblers, "reduce teenage pregnancies?" It was too early to parade statistics, but Lenny and Jessica were awed by the creative thinking and the boldness of the experiments. They were quick to applaud anyone who had the courage to try to solve stubborn social problems, the results of which, their jobs dealt with every day. The late thirties were further pressure-cooked by Hitler's rise to power, his threats to invade the countries of Europe and his quickly expanding efforts to outlaw and persecute the Jews.

Jessica, still yearning to recreate her life with Lenny, at night, in dreams, used Jonathan, now going through similar learning experiences. She was glad that he was blossoming, but the abrupt hiatus in his letter-writing worried her. At work during the day she closed the door on dire thoughts of what might have caused him to forget or delay writing, but asleep, her guard was down. On this night, her inmost thoughts broke loose in a display that her fears of losing the second man in her life blew up to frightening proportions...

She saw Jonathon standing alone against the sky in the vast sands of the Negev. "Jonathan, what are you doing out there alone? Where's

Jimmy?"

"He's at the *Kibbutz*."

"Why did you separate? You'd agreed to travel together."

"He was intrigued by this particular kibbutz. He thought Jews in Israel were…all Jewish, but he discovered that eighty percent of Israelis don't care about ancient ritual that doesn't bear on today's problems."

"Why are you walking in the Negev? It's dangerous. Do you have water?"

"I'm looking for something."

"Yes, Jonathan, I know. You miss your dad. I understand that. Lenny took a part of me, too, when he went. But you're twenty, on the verge of creating your own life. You'll find ways to make up for missing parts. I'm not saying that because I think it's easy, but it's what you…we…everyone has to do."

Suddenly Emily Karelin was running between them, but running in loose sand wastes energy and she tired quickly. Exhausted, panting, she lifted one foot heavily forward and then the other. Jessica wanted to ask her what happened to the Lee baby, but saw that Emily was distressed enough, and Jessica hadn't finished talking to Jonathan. She moved to one side to look past Emily slugging her way through the sand. "Jonathan, Jonathan," she called to his retreating figure.

"What, Mom, what?"

Jessica could no longer see him, but hoped he could hear. "For me, it's not just about losing Lenny, but your sister, who didn't make it into our world. I had to find ways…I look for ways to make up for her. The agency, Jonno, is more than…just work at the agency. I hope you find it…if it isn't Poly Sci, well, at your age, Jonno, you have time…

Jessica saw him leaning over the thin, tubular rail of a small motor launch that bounced him into the waves, splashing heavy spray over him. Jessica worried that he was getting a soaking that would seriously chill him.

Jonathan threw his head back and laughed uproariously at the sudden deluge. Water matted his long hair, pasted it around his head and face. "Jonathan," Jessica called to him, but he was enjoying the sea too much to answer. Another wave broke over him. With another burst of laughter he waved vigorously to her. Jessica couldn't decide whether he was calling for help or waving goodbye. He was more interested in laughing than answering her call.

"Answer me, Jonathan," she spoke with the pain of being ignored.

The boat bounced and pitched from wave to wave, Jonathon got smaller and smaller, his laughter fainter. There was no rope to hold him this time. Jessica felt an emptiness. She weakly raised her hand a bit to wave, in a vain thought to connect...

The ache of her repeated loss woke her again. The warm dampness on her pillow told her she'd been crying.

Before breakfast, Jessica sat in front of her mirror holding small ice packs on her eyes, and remembered her worries of the night about Jonathan's missing letter. *I could phone this Kibbutz Revi and find out if he's still there. But an international phone call, to a kibbutz in the desert...find the person who had contact with him...* Jessica shook her head at the difficulties.

The chill of the icepacks calmed her. Sitting there, organizing her thoughts for the day ahead, she unexpectedly made a decision about the Liebman adoption. It happened so suddenly, she felt stunned. "Huh!" she said aloud as the unexpected resolution struck her. Even though she thought she might be grabbing onto her conclusion as much out of impatience as conviction, she hurried through dressing and into the kitchen for a heartier than usual breakfast, adding an egg and slice of toast to orange juice, oatmeal and tea. *If all has gone well with the Liebman's second visit, yes!*

In her office at the first meeting of the day, Jessica couldn't help smiling at Roberta and Emily in response to the little-girl song in her head, '*A secret, a secret, I have a secret.*' "How'd it go yesterday, Emily?" Jessica asked.

Emily took a moment to think and formulate her reply. A shrug of her shoulders, a slight shake of her head and a look of surprise was on her face before she said, "Yes, Jessica, yes, it...it went well."

"It surprised you?"

"Yes, it surprised me."

"Why?"

"These are White people, *ofays*." Emily saw the questioning frown on Jessica's face. "That's pig-Latin for 'foe'; Watts talk," she explained, "but they had no difficulty relating to Lee." Emily stopped to think more about it. "It wasn't phoney. Amy, the daughter, sang to him."

Smiling, Jessica nodded and then asked Roberta, "How was your interview with Amy?"

Roberta's face was thoughtful. Her lips pursed. "Amy is an unusual youngster."

"Unusual, positive?"

"Oh yes. Like her parents, she has daily contact with other races." Roberta felt the need to express it more firmly. "Yes," she said, agreeing with Emily, "it seems to be genuine."

In the silence Emily and Roberta watched feelings chase each other across Jessica's face; a pleasant smile and a nod, a tensing of her lips, a tightening of her jaw, then her head lowered until her eyes looked directly into Emily's, and then Roberta's. "We-ell," Jessica began, the slow clarity of that word like a bell announcing the start of battle, "there doesn't seem to be any reason why the adoption process shouldn't continue." She looked at each of them again, this time silently questioning them for their response.

A tiny, impulsive gasp from Roberta.

Emily nodded thoughtfully in agreement.

Still silent, Roberta's pale blue eyes widened as if trying to signal to Jessica about the troubling legal questions.

Jessica continued. "Steve Gorelni said yes to our continuing the interview process." She noted the surprised confusion on Roberta's face, but went on. "With the favorable reports from the two of you, I see no reason why we shouldn't call the Liebmans and tell them we're going to give them the Lee baby, when he's eight months old as usual."

Roberta's restrained objections destroyed the placid

professionalism of her face. Her tone was hurt, aloof. "But, Jessica...there is a law..."

"I'm expecting Steve to do something about that."

"That...that won't be easy. What if he can't?"

Jessica's hands sprang from her desk into the air in a gesture of finality. "Tough."

Emily smiled.

Roberta stared in consternation. "*Tough*?"

"Look at what that law has done to us as an agency; flooded us with 'unadoptable' babies, and we can't find enough proper foster homes. Babies, in the most needy time of their lives, are improperly cared for. That law is defeating our purpose as a *child-placement* bureau." Aware that she was battering them, Jessica pulled back, took time for a deep breath and continued more quietly. "When I came in this morning, I'd already determined that, having unwillingly donated another night of sleep to the job... enough! I *have* to do the *sane* thing."

A conscious part of Jessica's decision that morning was that she was not going to get upset when she talked to Roberta and Emily. While she felt exhilarated by her courage, swiping away thirty-two years of unquestioned conforming to agency guidelines, left Jessica soloing in a singular, frightening freedom.

When she started the Liebman processing, she sensed that she couldn't, emotionally and administratively, stand alone in this and sought Roberta's supporting hand, to the restrained extent that support was available. Now, looking at Roberta's clouded face, Jessica knew that, administratively, on a supervisory level, she was *totally* alone in this decision. Jessica felt her pulse racing. She breathed deeply and exhaled abruptly.

Roberta stiffened. "Jessica," she started, her lips in quiet, tense restraint, "if we give Lee to the Liebmans, and the law is not changed, the baby could legally be taken away from them, adding to Lee's traumas..."

"And I could be forced to resign for ignoring guidelines!" Compulsively, that sentence flew out of Jessica's need to tell her employees, the agency, everyone in Sacramento, *I believe in what I'm doing that much, that I'm willing to resign over it!*

The thought of Jessica's unequivocal resignation jolted Roberta and Emily upright.

This was impending Armageddon.

Under better control, Jessica continued. "Ladies, after another sleepless night, I made a decision. If the interviewing process continues positive, the Liebmans get the Lee baby. That's what we're here for. If the powers that be decide that I've committed an illegal act and ask for my resignation, so be it."

Jessica waited for a response, but Emily and Roberta were in shock. Sure of her comprehension of the agency statistics, Jessica quoted quietly, "If these children are allowed to go to homes that ask for them, seventy percent of this agency's problems would disappear."

"But, Jessica," Roberta protested, as close to sputtering helplessly as Jessica had ever seen her, "we...we don't have families asking for them."

Jessica smiled, imagining her son Jonathon, home for a rare dinner, slapping the table and declaring to her, "Nice work, Mom!"

"I have faith," Jessica said, "once it gets known. We've never thought to ask how many people are out there who feel like the Liebmans, that having a baby to care for is more important than the baby's origin." She smiled at her feeling of a growing attachment to her son, no matter what direction his energies hurled him. Also, she was liking more and more what she was saying to Emily and Roberta, because it made her feel a rare harmony of thought and deed. Jessica stopped to relish it, to watch her intellect, principles and social work values race toward a unity with her feelings for those babies.

That internal amalgam she was unexpectedly displaying to her staff, to the world, transformed her. She sat up straight, grinning. Her eyes shone. She had a remembered image of nursing baby Jonathon. While he sucked, his eyes turned up to look at her. Jessica knew he wanted to smile his happiness at being connected to his mom, but he was too hungry to stop feeding.

Looking at Roberta and Emily, Jessica's decision summed up not only a rare moment of setting a vision for her staff, but the validation it brought to her thirty-two years. Suddenly suffused, as with a religious experience, she leaned forward to the two and, with all of who she was, and all that she stood for, she whispered, "A baby in a home is a *miracle.*"

Despite her troubling restraints, Roberta was awed by Jessica's ecstasy.

Inspired to be told again why she chose childcare as a career, Emily's face shone in response.

Jessica had said what was on her heart. Feeling as close to being sanctified as she ever had, she sat back slowly and waited.

After a moment, Emily spoke, slowly, thoughtfully. "I talked with Reverend Pearson, pastor of my church. I was troubled…in the beginning…about a Negro baby going to a White home, being raised in a White neighborhood."

Surprised, Jessica asked, "You were?"

"Yes."

"You didn't say anything to me."

"No, because I wasn't sure. My boyfriend Philip works with the Watts Improvement Committee. The WIC believes in building Watts economically and culturally. We can't do that if our babies are given away outside our community…"

"But Watts families are not asking for babies."

"I know that. That's what I told Philip. I even took him to talk with Reverend Pearson, who's also part of WIC. Philip finally agreed that babies need homes *now,* White or whatever, as long as it's a loving home."

"Well said." Jessica breathed, and looked at Roberta.

Roberta stiffened. She spoke haltingly, quietly. "Of course…I agree, Jessica, but we… do have a legal obstacle."

Jessica nodded in agreement. "Yes, we do." She paused to consider how to explain to these two, the dream-filled, restless nights that resulted in her epiphany. "I've learned something in thirty-two years, Roberta, Emily. If I can't apply what I've learned in my years of work, I'm not for that job…and the job description is not for me."

Jessica felt tears welling in her eyes. She blinked hard. *Not now, not now, Jessica, you're still the director. It's still your agency.* Jessica's chin tilted up. "I don't want to live a lie anymore. I need to do what I believe. If the politicians don't agree..." Jessica raised her hands and dropped them in acceptance of her decision. "...Sorry." Emily's lips were trembling. "You're...you're thinking of resigning, Jessica?"

Jessica shook her head to tell Emily she would not initiate it. "If they insist," she said, and then repeated it emphatically, "*only* if they insist."

"That...that would be...a terrible loss, Jessica."

"Thank you, Emily."

Wounded, but not responding in anger, Roberta asked quietly, "How...how shall we proceed, Jessica?"

Cleansed to the point of being light-headed, Jessica smiled to Roberta. "Call the Liebmans and tell them we're going ahead with the adoption."

Roberta's face clouded.

Jessica feared she would cry. She tried to help her. "You are only the messenger, Roberta. *I* penned the message. I take full, *all,* responsibility for it."

But Roberta felt roughly torn from her life's framework, and was unable to respond for the moment. She wilted. Though Jessica had absolved her of any wrongdoing, she sat.

Emily turned her head to look curiously at Roberta.

Jessica spoke quietly. "We've known for a long time how cruel it is for these children...*any* children...to be shuttled from one foster home to another, even if they're good ones, *the child doesn't belong anywhere!* At eighteen, he's ejected into a world that taught him there's no place for him. I don't want...any longer...*can't* be part of it. I feel guilty accepting a system that does this."

Jessica looked at Roberta. Her head was down. She seemed to be suffering. "Last year the Supreme Court said that segregation is illegal. Yet we are still living with a law that segregates." Jessica shook her head, threw up her hands and whispered with a sob, "I can't do this anymore."

There was a long silence while each wrestled with her own brink of tears.

Finally, Roberta struggled out of her chair, whispering, "I'll...call them." She left, closing the door quietly behind her.

Emily asked, "Is that all, Jessica?"

"Yes."

Emily left.

Jessica sat. Turbulence prevented her from functioning. She'd looked at the worst that could happen. But that was in the presence of her assistant and staff worker. Alone, some realities set in. The emptiness of life-without-the-agency was revealed to her. It felt like walking to the edge of a cliff and looking down, *All of worth has been taken from me and it's time to consider...* Appalled at her thoughts, she straightened, as if pulling back from the edge, then argued for her new self. Of w*hat good is an agency that's running scared* before the whips of the rednecks, contorting ourselves to live within the ridiculous strictures they yoke us with? Jessica shook her head, again rejecting such an unworkable premise. "It's senseless!"

Yet, amazed at her willingness to precipitate such a radical life-change, on her own, *without* Lenny, Jessica suddenly grinned. This was her first statement of direction without feeling the need to ask herself, *What would Lenny say?* She gasped at the miracle of it. *All on my own!* Kicking off burdens that had been denied a solution because the legislature didn't think them of importance, she felt light headed. Yet only just born to freedom, she felt as unknowing as an infant. She grasped at it as a way of cementing her relationship with her son. *Wait tll I tell Jonno.* Hoping to steady herself in her new way of life, she slapped a hand on the edge of her desk, her usual expression for, *Glad I made that decision,* and tried to laugh.

Chapter 12

Amy and George were home when the phone rang. "Mr. Liebman, this is Miss Walker."

George thought her voice more constrained than usual. "Yes, Miss Walker."

"We're going ahead with the adoption, Mr. Liebman."

"Wonderful!"

"We do have to keep the baby until he's eight months old to complete his testing."

"Yes, we understand that."

"You can expect to pick him up in three months."

"Very good! Thank you!"

"Will the bedrooms be ready?"

"Oh yes. The driveway will be asphalted this week and Hank and I will be closing up the bedroom walls next week."

"Good. Then you can pick him up on March 22nd, his eight-month birthday."

Three-and-a-half months away, thought George. That ought to give Hank and me time enough to finish everything, even with work going slower in the winter. "Very good. Thank you, Miss Walker." George cradled the phone. "We're getting the baby, Amy."

"Great!"

"A name, a name, Amy. We have to think of a name."

"A Chinese name?"

"He looks more Chinese than anything."

The Liebmans knew nothing about a Chinese name, one that would be appropriate. *For a Chinese-Negro baby?* George had written and produced *Kwe-Ling and the Fishermen* in *Dance Center's* studio/theater, set in the time of Mandarin culture. In preparation he'd read many folk tales, poems and stories of Chinese operas. He recalled the names he selected for the play's characters, but decided they were too foreign-sounding for an American boy. It would tend to separate him from his friends. *Born in LA,* thought George, *he's an American citizen.* George wondered how to say Chinese-American in Chinese.

After she called the Liebmans, Roberta sat, overwhelmed, wrestling with Jessica's, *I penned the message, Roberta, I am the only one responsible for this.* Roberta tightened her lips. *Doesn't she realize that it affects me too?* Roberta had moved from her scattered county in Kansas to the denser Los Angeles, where social work was more visibly important to an expanding population. Thrilled to have been promoted to Jessica's assistant, her career was advancing as wished. *Of course, we're all sympathetic to our clients...Will those men in Sacramento listen to her?* She suddenly realized that one of them did. *Well, Mr. Gorelni told her to continue the processing.* Roberta shook her head in wonder and admiration. *She's...she has courage.*

The following Sunday was cloudy and cold. The unfriendly weather gave George the excuse he needed to postpone his working on the deck. "How about a Chinese dinner?" he proposed to Lil and Amy.

They agreed. "And we can ask the waiter about a Chinese name for the baby," Amy said.

"Great idea," said George.

They had dinner at their favorite Chinese restaurant, *Chung Mee.* After the meal, George beckoned the waiter to the table. "We're adopting a Chinese-American boy and we'd like to give him a Chinese name. How do you say *Chinese-American* in Chinese?"

Puzzled, the waiter looked at George. "You...get...Chinese boy?"

George nodded. "Yes." He gestured to include Amy and Lil. "We're adopting him. We'd like to give him a Chinese name. How do you say *Chinese-American* in Chinese?"

"Chinese-Amelican? Dat's Mee-Wah."

George tried it out silently, then thought perhaps *American* should be first. "Can you say, *Wah-Mee?*"

The waiter grimaced thoughtfully. "Ye-ah…you can say."

"How do you say *joyous*?"

The waiter frowned, puzzled.

"*Joyous, happy,*" George explained.

The waiter's face cleared. "Oh, *happy.* Happy is *huan.*"

"Thank you. Thank you very much."

The waiter smiled. "Yes." He nodded, and walked away.

Her blue eyes shining to try it, Amy sounded it out. "Mee-Wah, Mee-wah Liebman.

"Yeah," she grinned, "he looks like a Mee-Wah."

Smiling, Lil was nodding in agreement. "My adult class is dying to throw a welcome party for him. I'll tell Jeannette and Helen it's going to happen." Lil turned to George. "We need to find time to shop. A crib, a high-chair, diapers."

"You don't have any baby furniture from Amy?"

"Heavens, no. One of the parents at Amy's pre-school had a baby and I lent her the crib and high chair." Smiling at how long ago it was, Lil shook her head. "I can't even remember who it was."

George thought of the affluent homes of some of Lil's dance students. "I'll bet some of your adult students would be glad to lend us baby stuff they're not using."

"Sure. I'll ask."

After her Monday morning class, when Lil told her students they were getting the baby, students promised not only a crib and a high-chair, but a stroller, a small table on wheels, a rocking horse and a tricycle. Lil asked them to hold off bringing the items to class until the bedrooms were ready.

"Diaper service, Lil, you've *got* to have diaper service!" said Elise, who had just gotten her twins potty-trained out of their diapers.

"Yes," agreed Helen. "Elise, take pledges."

The list of pledges from the students guaranteed three months of diaper service. Overwhelmed, Lil thanked everyone. Jeannette and Helen asked Lil to stay on for a while to help plan the welcome party.

Since the Liebmans were getting the baby on March 22nd, Jeannette and Helen set the party date for the last Friday in March, the 30th. Lil called the diaper service from the studio office and told them to start delivering on March 21st. Relieved that so many baby concerns would be taken care of, Lil felt exuberant. She thanked them all for their help and hugged Jeannette and Helen.

The next morning George bundled himself into his warm jacket against the damp cold and met with the paving company foreman at the bottom of the hill. They measured off the distance from the top of the Ewing Street cul-de-sac, along the upward curve that George had dug with a rented tractor, to the end of the deck of the house. They agreed on a price for the ten-foot wide driveway and the job was set for Friday.

When George got back in the house the phone was ringing. "Hello, I'm Martin Peters, reporter for the *LA Times.* I'd like to interview you and Mrs. Liebman and your daughter."

"Oh? Why?"

"You're adopting an inter-racial child, aren't you?"

"Yes."

"You're a Caucasian family?

"Yes."

"I think it's a story."

George was about to ask *why* again, but stopped himself. Someone wanting to throw open to the public what George thought was a private family matter, *Even if,* he mused, *no one else thought of doing it...but then,* he smiled, still holding the phone, *isn't that the way with us contrarians...Damn!* he interrupted his own thought with annoyance, *What's so unusual about asking for a child of any national origin? Only in America is that a problem...no, that's not true...White superiority flourishes in Europe too. World War II finished Hitler but not racism. He rephrased it more accurately. Only in a White world would this adoption get their backs up.*

Peters broke into the long silence. "Mr. Liebman?"

"Still here, thinking about it. I'm catching up to why this is such

a big deal, in a country that proclaims '*All men are created equal*'."
George smiled, pleased with his smart-ass tactic of pretending *naïveté*
to make his point.

"You're not serious."

"About what?"

"About telling me that you don't think your request is unusual.
This is a country that profited by running slaves for two hundred
years. We're still suffering a racist hangover." Peters paused, then
asked, "And you didn't think you were tearing up a few sacred
practices? Are you pulling my leg?"

"Am I?

"I can't believe that you thought you were making an innocent
adoption request," Peters' voice heated up, "certainly not in America,
not in California. You had to know you were rattling sacred icons."

Peters made George aware that the publicity would create
obstacles to the adoption. *Of course Peters is right.* George shifted
gears. He hunkered down once again in his familiar political foxhole
to figure out his next guerilla tactics. "I'm not sure," he began, "that
I want to blast it to them on loudspeakers or hold a headline against
their noses, and shake them up so they can have time to stop it."

"It could be a great story."

George felt reaffirmed that the families who enthusiastically
applauded the intercultural programs of *Dance Center* and signed
their kids up for Lil's and his classes, lived on the side of sanity. But
outside the cultural oasis he and Lil created, Peters' interview would
tell those who'd be emotionally violated if a Negro sat in their home
and ate dinner with them, that with the adoption, something similar
was taking place, and with the blessing of *their* State of California.

Again in the political trenches, debating what tactic would carry
the adoption forward, George asked himself again, *Will the interview
help or hurt?* He shook his head. *Lil and I and Amy made the adoption
request because we wanted a baby, period. But a White home taking
in a dark-skinned child doesn't go down without being noticed 'out
there.'* George suddenly realized that the parents and children who
took classes at *Dance Center,* came to the bi-monthly Family Nights,

where adults and children folk-danced together, and attended weekend concert performances by Odetta, Pete Seeger, Crescencio Ruiz, the African students...productions of American, Celtic, Mexican, African, Israeli and Balkan cultures. He remembered dark-skinned Jess Dumas saying to him at a *Dance Center* Family Night, "You know, George, this is the only place in LA, I can bring my White wife and my inter-racial children for a relaxed evening."

What's the big deal? George thought. A baby needs a home. We offer ours, and it's a problem, a lightning flash in an arid forest, and all the vermin hiding under the dry leaves are screaming in protest. Too bad the word got out. George asked Peters, "How did you find out?"

"Reporters keep in touch."

"Yeah." *If Americans were really treated as equals,* George's mind ran on, silently mocking the establishment yet again, unable to stop venting his anger at its verbal hypocrisies, *this would be a simple A-B-C event; couple wants a baby, baby needs parents, couple gets baby.* But George knew that equation didn't prove out for most Americans, especially those in power. The higher up, the less agreeable to George's way of life. *You don't do anything to darken White skin,* was their credo. With sardonic pride, he thought, *Contrarian Liebman against the tide again, but at a price, as usual.* Fear of being denied kicked him in the gut. *The ruckus it creates might be big enough so we don't get the baby.*

"Hello? Mr. Liebman?"

Is he going to be friend or foe? George wondered. "Yeah," George said shakily, "I'm here. I'll...I'll ask my wife and my daughter. Can I get back to you...uh...late this afternoon?"

"Sure."

George wrote down the reporter's name, office and home numbers and hung up. Glad the grinding pressure that dredged up so much, was over, he let out his breath and cradled the phone. His arm hurt from his tension of holding the receiver. He opened and closed his fingers to relieve the stress of it, then shook his arm to relax it.

The Liebmans hadn't booked for the fuss and fury. George sat, trying to think his way to the top of it. *The LA Times is conservative. Why are they interested in this? Or, are they? Maybe Peters is doing this on his own? I'll ask him when I talk to him.*

When Lil and Amy came home from the studio George told them about the interview request. Lil thought an interview could be good; unexpected PR for *Dance Center*. Amy was excited about getting her name in the paper.

"Maybe, maybe not," George cautioned. "You remember that *Life Magazine* did a photo story of our wedding, a dancer's wedding, choreographed by Zemach, but we ended up on the cutting room floor; not Hollywood enough."

George called Peters back. "How soon do you want to do this?"

"Tomorrow, if possible."

George wanted to give the interview his best, not squeezed between work schedules of house building, teaching and road paving. He scanned the coming days for one when all three Liebmans could give it time. "I don't think we're free until the weekend."

"Saturday?"

"No. Lil teaches all day Saturday. Sunday afternoon?"

"Fine."

George gave Peters the address and told him how to drive to the house.

When George opened the door, he thought Martin Peters was older than his young voice had indicated. He wore a jacket, but his shirt collar was unbuttoned and no tie. His brown hair was graying. The lines from his nostrils to the corners of his mouth were fleshy and noticeable. Casual *a la* LA, but not the stereotype of the brash reporter George had preconceived. After the four were seated, George started back at square one. "How did you hear about this?"

"The *Times* Sacramento office phoned us."

"Sacramento! What's Sacramento got to do with this?"

Peters gave George a 'You've got to be kidding' look. But then, seeing George's blank expression, he caught on that the family really didn't realize what they had stirred up. Peters explained patiently to all three Liebmans. He felt he was back teaching *Journalism 101* at UCLA. "The LA County Bureau of Adoptions is a branch of the State Bureau of Adoptions in Sacramento. Any change in regulations has to be referred to Sacramento. Last week there was a phone call from the LA office saying they were considering a change."

"What change?" Lil asked.

"A Negro child was being considered for a White home."

"Is that so inconceivable?" Lil asked.

George smiled to himself. The reporter was raising the hair on Lil's neck like Peters' call had done to him.

"No and yes," Peters said, "but it would defy the law. Steve Gorelni, director of the State Bureau of Adoption, submitted a request to the Health and Human Services Committee of state legislature to change the law. Our *Times* legislative reporter wired a squib to the LA office. Meanwhile, conservative legislators passed the word to *The John Birch Society...*"

"What!" George exploded, "what do *they* have to do with an adoption?"

"Nothing, officially. But their politicians have pounded the legislative table insisting that Negro children go to Negro homes and White children to White homes, and they define inter-racial children as 'non-White'... They don't want the races mixed. As you know, they've succeeded so far."

Well, thought George, silently venting his cynicism, *we go along doing the decent thing, harming no one, but the establishment regulars are screaming, "It poisons America!"*

Eisenhower warned us about the reactionary military-industrial complex running the country, but down to this, adopting a baby? Again facing the corporate monster, George felt fragile. He bolstered himself by remembering Rosa Parks. *She did a job on the establishment down in segregation land. The Montgomery bus boycott is big in the national media. She's got enough courage to throw us some in California.* George looked at Peters. "The legislature could stop the adoption."

Peters' shrug seemed to express his neutrality. "It could go either way."

George looked at Lil. Her cynicism about equality in America was even stronger than his. Born in France, she was brought to America when she was six. During the McCarthy hearings, the Department of Immigration questioned Lil for possible deportation. Fortunately she was able to produce her citizenship papers. She placed the precious original in the hands of Attorney Jordan, a *Dance Center* board member. He made copies for the government and locked the original in his office safe. *Why the insinuated threat of deportation?* George asked himself, seeking clarification, *because her work connecting many cultures is not American? Because we created and produced the first inter-racial singing quartet in LA with Sue Matsuma, Odetta, Ernie Lieberman and Jan Berry?*

George sat dumbfounded, kicked out of innocence again by the political reaction to their request for a mixed baby. He shook his head disbelieving what they'd set off. *A simple request. Hardly subversive, but it upset the racist pattern that powerful people want to retain in America. Lil threatened with deportation?* George trembled as if he'd just received a subpoena from the House Unamerican Activities Committee. *I see what we got into. Why did I ever think it was an innocent request?*

He turned to Lil to see how she was taking it. She was looking at George with a cynical smirk that said, 'As usual, the reactionaries are pulling our strings.'

George saw Amy look questioningly at Lil, then at him, but grappling with the impact of Peters' statement, George had to put off explaining to her. *Have we kicked open a hornet's nest? Are we prone to get stung? Could we lose seven years of community cultural work?* George recalled turning down Westinghouse's offer to become an engineer because it felt awkward to think of giving up theater activity. *I'm where I want to be. When I met Lil in LA after the war, she convinced me to work at theater full time, because this is what I really love to do.*

Peters, savvy reporter, waited, didn't push ahead to get the answers to his prepared questions.

George sat back and scanned seven years of *Dance Center*. Dance, well-taught in its intercultural context, makes people feel better about themselves, connects peoples across national barriers. Remembering a joke around the studio, he smiled. 'If Generals learned to dance, there'd be no more wars.' *If they stop this adoption because of racism, America's a liar.* George had been there before. Confounded, he looked at Peters. *Nice guy, but the bringer of bad news.* George took a deep breath. *Well, here we go again. The John Birchers say what Lil and I do is a no-no. Damn right it's not their way!* His anger, however, did not steady his trembling. George looked at Peters, the next question he wanted to ask threatened to blow the top of his head; *"So who listens to the extreme right?"* But Peters had already answered it. "Politicians." Conservative clout in the legislature could stop the adoption.

Powerlessness against the paid-for power of regressive politicians was the feeling that George hated most. On the corrupt anvil of big money buying legislative clout, America's ideal of 'all men are created equal' is smashed to a shapeless pulp. Only the buyers of politicians count. George could understand corporate opposition to labor union demands and paying their legislative lackeys to beat down bills protecting union rights, or raising the minimum wage, but denying a baby a home? Powerlessness, endemically joined-at-the-hip to failure, made George feel sick.

Peters waited until he sensed the debris from their emotional shock had settled sufficiently to carry on. He looked from George, to Lil, to Amy and to George again. Holding his notepad and pen, he spoke quietly. "May I ask you some questions?"

George nodded.

"I heard that you teach children of all races."

George smiled wearily. "Yes, we do, unAmerican as it is."

Peters acknowledged the sarcasm with a small smile.

George and Lil responded to a run of the reporter's questions that sought out the kind of people they were, and the kind of things they did, plus more of what George had been through with Miss Walker. While Peters was writing his shorthand, George thought of the question he'd had in mind before the interview; *Is Peters doing this on his own, or did the Times assign him?* With the new information, however, that the impending adoption was shaking political security blankets in Sacramento, *any* newspaper, on the right or left, would want the story, for their own purpose.

"What's the *Times* editorial opinion on this?" George asked.

"Not my department," was Peters' instant answer. Then, after a pause, his tone was more considered. "I don't know which side they'll come down on in this, if they give it editorial space at all." Peters rattled off his reporter's familiarity with the Adoption Bureau's situation. "The social-work profession is up to its eyeballs with mixed babies of teen mothers. There aren't enough foster homes. Conditions in some are shocking. No Negro families are asking to adopt them and White families are not encouraged to ask because of the law. So White families don't ask, until yours did."

George wondered why Peters did the summation. *Camouflage to avoid being put on the spot for a personal opinion? Is he refusing to speculate with us for fear of legal backlash?* George tried to keep Peters vocalizing. "Which way do you think this might go?"

But talking off the cuff was not what Peters came for. He double-checked his question list. Satisfied he'd done them all, he slipped his notepad and pen into his jacket pocket, and stood up.

"Well, thanks," he said. "It'll be interesting to see how it comes out. And…" he reached his hand toward George and they shook. "Good luck." He turned his head to include Lil and Amy, "to all of you. Thanks again." And he was gone.

The Liebmans were left in a wretched silence. George raised his hands in a gesture, but unable to say anything, he dropped them again. Out on the deck the stack of large second-hand windows were waiting for him to be installed, to begin the work of turning the deck into an enclosed porch, and Sunday was usually a day for working on the house. But George's muscles ached in response to seeing the stacked windows, and it was December. *It's cold out there. Not today. Enough.*

Monday afternoon, driving home from work, Jessica worried about Jonathan. The last she'd heard was that he and Danny had boarded a ship in Greece, sailing for Marseilles via the Mediterranean. *As long as they stay in Southern Europe,* thought Jessica, *they won't freeze to death.* But one letter had talked of their determination to make it to Paris before heading home.

My kid was born and raised in LA. He doesn't know what a real winter's like. He doesn't have that kind of clothing with him.

At home there was no letter from Jonathan. Frustrated by her not having any way to write, call or telegram him, Jessica washed her few dinner dishes and went to bed.

A ringing phone in the middle of the night startled her awake. She turned on the lamp and looked at the clock. One-forty. "Hello."

"Hello, Mom. Can you pick us up at the airport?"

"Jonathan! Airport? What airport?"

"LA, LA, Mom. We're home. United Airlines, gate…"

"It's almost two o'clock in the morning."

"I know, Mom, we're beat. It was a turbulent crossing. We hardly slept at all."

"Take a taxi."

"We don't have the money…"

"Take a bus. Change for the one that comes up La Cienega Boulevard…"

"Mom, please."

"Why didn't you tell me you were coming home?"

"There wasn't time. We ran into a killer blizzard just before Paris. We had to book immediate passage to London to get out of there. We owe Travelers' Aid eighteen dollars and fifty-two cents for our tickets. If it hadn't been for them we'd still be huddled around the stove in a bus station south of Paris. The blizzard stopped and the sky cleared, but the temp was barely above zero."

"Are you all right?"

"Yeah, beat, dead."

"Is Jimmy all right?"

"Yeah."

Jessica decided twenty-four hours of sleep would restore them. They could start now at the airport. "Jonathan, I'm not getting up in the middle of the night and driving out there. Sleep where you are. I'll pick you up before I go to work. What waiting room are you in?"

"United."

"Incoming, ticket desk?"

"Yeah."

"Sleep well."   ·

"Thanks."

Jessica reached over and cradled the phone, but continuing to sit up, she found herself smiling. *He's home, the biggest worry off my mind. And I didn't fall for his mommy-I-need-help dramatization. Treat him like an adult and he'll act like an adult. He's home in time to register for the January quarter.* Jessica determined that by the end of the week he'd be back in Berkley applying to finish his second year.

That pleased with herself, she was still smiling as she scooted down under the covers, snuggled onto her side and drew her knees up.

By Wednesday, all of Jonathan's facilities returned to normal. Jessica looked at her son's relaxed body slumped comfortably in his chair after a good dinner. The European winter hadn't erased the bronze color the Israeli sun had burned into his face. It made a handsome combination with his brown eyes and longish black hair. Jessica had a sudden thought. *What if Jonathan's bronze were darker, and permanent, like the baby Lee's color? Would I be as comfortable calling him my son, loving him?* She thought about it. *The Liebmans,* Jessica decided, *act as it they've been through that self-search and came up with a positive answer.* Jessica shook her head. *Not usually done. I have to admire them.*

Jessica's thoughts returned to Jonathan. He'd just finished his second night of airing his excitement about his trip. She knew that his seeing Europe ten years after the most devastating war in history had to mature his perspective. He'd talked about rubble piles still in many streets, and ruined walls with holes in them like gaping eye sockets in skulls, still standing. A coastal ship that the boys had sailed on carried a full load of food supplies for central Europe, under America's Marshall plan.

Looking at the cluttered table between them, Jessica smiled to herself. *But some things don't change.* The chaos of emptied and part-emptied dishes, so annoying to her, as always, did not offend her son. "Clear, Jonathan," she said.

He looked up frowning, not understanding her command.

"Clear the table."

"Oh. Yeah." He started his reluctant getting up.

"And then we'll talk."

Half-way, he stopped. After two evenings of talking and answering his mother's questions, he felt all talked out. "Oh? What about?"

"Getting back to school."

"Oh. Yeah."

Balancing a part of the dish mess on his hands, he started his trek to the sink.

He's not twenty-one until March twentieth, Jessica thought gratefully. *Until then, he won't even think of asking about his trust fund.* She was glad too, that she and Lenny had earmarked it *for furthering his education only. Lots of experiences could be considered as 'furthering one's education'. So far, he understands that it means formal education. There's enough in the fund to carry him through a PhD, if he ever latches on to something that grabs him.* "Don't run the dishwasher," she said.

"Okay."

Jonathan sat down at the cleared table.

"There's enough money in your trust fund to carry you through a PhD…"

"In what?"

"You tell me."

Jonathan looked at his mother. He nodded. "Yeah."

"But first things first. Call the school and arrange to get back into classes." Jessica saw him bridle. "You agreed to finish two years," she said firmly.

Jonathan grimaced. "Yeah, okay."

"Then we can talk about whether it's worth your continuing or not."

In bed, just before turning off her lamp, Jessica thought sadly, *I'm still pushing it for him. When does he pick it up and run with it?*

Chapter 13

Monday, driving to lunch, Jessica was especially appreciative of the balmy spring weather. The warmth, unexpected for mid-March, the sunlight, the new young leaves...all combined to soothe Jessica's jitters, but only *some*. The adoption was going ahead. On Friday, she'd instructed Roberta to tell the Liebmans they could pick up their baby on the coming Thursday. She still hadn't heard anything further from Steve. She assumed...hoped...that he'd arranged whatever had to be arranged so neither he nor she would be called in for flaunting California law.

At Friday's meeting, not being able to tell Roberta that the Health and Human Services Committee of the state legislature had given the adoption its blessing, had caused tension between them. Roberta's lips seemed more tightly compressed. She sat more stiffly upright in her chair, and wrote unnecessarily on her pad to avoid meeting Jessica's eyes. Jessica's instruction to call the Liebmans and tell them they can pick up their baby on the following Thursday made Roberta shudder as if she'd been hit, but she kept her eyes down and wrote it on her pad. Jessica thought of repeating that Roberta had no culpability in the decision, no matter what reaction occurred. Jessica decided it was of no use. She knew Roberta would call and get it done, but also knew that she'd lost a friend. *And how will it be working with her?*

Stopped for the light, Jessica shook her head. *No matter how much I tell her that I bear all responsibility for this, she can't relax. She acts as if I've handcuffed her and I'm sending her off to jail.*

The light changed to green. Annoyed with Roberta, and with herself for not being able to convince her assistant to relax, simply carry out orders and enjoy the day, Jessica lost her clutch coordination and ground the gears. Despite the honks behind her, she stopped the car, deliberately shifted into first and took off again.

Their discomfort with each other at Friday's meeting had soured Jessica's weekend.

Going in on Monday, instead of feeling elated that something unusual...even extraordinary...was going to happen on Thursday, she felt burdened with possible consequences, including the loss of working camaraderie with her assistant, and not with the glory of the event itself. Jessica and Roberta had no further reason to meet on Monday, so Jessica left her office early for lunch to escape to the sunshine of the spring day.

At the agency Nancy took a long distance call.

"Mrs. Keebler please."

"She's not at her desk, sir."

"Where is she?"

"She's out to lunch."

"Do you know where she eats?"

"Well...yes..."

"Can you call the restaurant?"

"Is this an emergency, sir?"

"Of course it is!"

"Your name, sir?"

"Steve Gorelni."

"Oh, Mr. Gorelni." All agency switchboards in the state knew his name. "The message, sir."

"Find her. Tell her to phone me. I'll wait for her call."

"Thank you. Yes, sir."

Gorelni clicked off.

Normally lunch time was slow time at the agency, but under Gorelni's hammering Nancy's adrenaline shot up. Her hand was shaking as she ran a finger down the list of useful phone numbers taped to the shelf surface of the switchboard. She phoned *Phil's* restaurant.

The cashier's sweet voice wooed her. "Hello-o, Phil's."

"Please page Mrs. Jessica Keebler. It's an emergency."

Jessica was into her large salad with minimum dressing when

she heard, "Mrs. Jessica Keebler, please come to the cashier's phone."

Jessica stopped chewing and looked around. Evelyn, the cashier was holding the phone in one hand and beckoning frantically with the other. Unable to be heard above the full-house level of noise, Evelyn's eyes popped wide and her red lips were miming 'phone.'

Jessica groped for her purse, rose from the booth and worked her way around the noisy tables.

She took the phone from the cashier. "Thanks, Evelyn." Jessica stepped out of the line of patrons paying their tabs and leaned against the wall.

"Hello?"

"Jessica, Mr. Gorelni called. He said for you to call immediately. It's an emergency."

"Yes. Thank you, Nancy. I'll be right there."

Nancy clicked off. "Damn!" Jessica whispered. She handed the phone to Evelyn.

Annoyed that her relaxed lunch time was destroyed, she then worried about what Steve's emergency might be. "I have to run, Evelyn. I'll settle the bill tomorrow. Tell Henry to cancel my entree."

"Right."

Driving back to the agency, anxious Jessica tested possible scenarios, imagining herself summarily dismissed, then victorious with the Liebman adoption. She shook her head and angrily commanded herself to stop sweating the nonsense of fantasies, dire or triumphant.

At the agency she hurried up the long ramp of steps and pulled open the heavy glass door. "Get Mr. Gorlelni on the line, Nancy. I'll take it in my office."

Her phone was ringing as she pushed open her door. She parked her purse on the desk, picked up the phone and dropped into her chair. "Yes, Steve."

"I've read that you're going ahead with that Liebman placement."

"You've *read!*"

"Yes."

"Where?"

"*The Sacramento Sentinel.*"

"I didn't say anything to them or *anybody* outside the agency."

"They picked it up from the *LA Times.*"

"I didn't tell *them* anything either."

"Somebody did. Chairman of the Health Committee, McSweeny, called me to check the facts because Legislator Roy Ambrose is beating on him about *Somebody's breaking the law!* I countered by formally submitting a requested change in the law. Ambrose forced McSweeny to call an emergency meeting of the Health and Welfare Committee for tomorrow and you'd better be there!"

"*Me!* What do I...?"

"Someone's *got* to plead the case for what you're doing. No one can do it better than you. You're key to all of it. Under present law the adoption will be declared ill-advised and illegal. *You* could be *fired*, and perhaps *me* for not pulling the reins on you. You've *got* to get up here and plead your case. Call and get yourself on the morning shuttle to Sacramento."

Jessica's blood pressure was racing. She whispered, "Let...let me catch my breath, Steve."

"What? I can't hear you, Jessica."

"I...I'm thinking, Steve."

"It's past thinking, Jessica. That placement will never happen without you being here."

Jessica took several breaths.

Steve spoke into the long silence. "Jessica, while you're catching your breath, let me ask you a question. How come you went ahead, right to the brink..."

"Well, you said yes, process the family and you'd get back to me. Not hearing from you, I figured that you had taken care of whatever had to be taken care of."

"I may be your supervisor, Jessica, but I don't change the laws of California."   .

Jessica smiled to herself about her mini-deception. She realized she'd hoped she wouldn't hear from Steve once he said to continue with the process.

"I'd love to help you tomorrow, Jessica, but I'm setting up a weekend retreat with my staff." His voice rose with encouraging enthusiasm. "But I'm certainly with you in spirit. And so is McSweeny, chairman of the committee. We're lucky to have him on our side."

Jessica was sorting out what had to be done before she left. She'd calmed her turbulence enough to separate out the important from the unimportant. Suddenly, *I must tell Roberta* popped up in her mind. "Yes, yes," she affirmed into the phone.

"Jessica, did you say something?"

"...All...all right, Steve. I...I can manage it."

"Good. As soon as you make the flight arrangements, call me and I'll arrange for a page to pick you up at the airport."

"All right, Steve, I'll call you."

"Good luck, Jessica."

"Thanks, 'bye."

A ring to Roberta's office went unanswered. Jessica rang Nancy. "When Roberta comes in from lunch, Nancy,..."

"She's coming in the front door now."

"Tell her to come to my office."

"Yes, Jessica."

"Come in, Roberta, come in," Jessica said in answer to her knock. Roberta came in, a questioning look on her face.

Jessica's mind was whirling with what would be demanded of her facing the unknown in Sacramento. She couldn't quiet herself enough to edit her thoughts. She launched into a running narrative. "Steve called. I have to go to Sacramento to plead for a change in the laws. He's submitted a request to the Health and Human Services Committee. I'm leaving tomorrow morning." Jessica stopped to search Roberta's face for response." *She's focused, all ears.* "This could be what we've wanted, Roberta. It...could happen."

"You...you instructed me to tell the Liebmans that they could pick up their baby on Thursday, March 22nd. That's what I told them."

Jessica shook her head. "It's too soon, Roberta. With this new development...Before, I was willing to take my chances even if it meant resigning, but now it can happen *legally,* maybe."

"What should I tell the Liebmans?"

"Tell them it's postponed…to…to review the file. That's it, it's a first and I want to make sure that…that it's the right thing to do. Whatever seems right, Roberta."

Roberta, glad that she might be going *with* the law instead of against it, gave Jessica a small smile of relief. "I'll call them." She stood up, turned to leave but turned back. "I hope…Good luck, Jessica."

"Thanks, Roberta.

Roberta went to her office and called immediately. "Mr. Liebman, there's going to be a delay. You will not be picking up the baby on Thursday."

"What! Why?"

"The director of the agency wants to review the file."

"Mrs. Keebler?"

"Yes."

"Is there a problem?"

"Well, no…that is, not as far as you and Mrs. Liebman are concerned."

George waited. His mind tumbled with what might be happening. *News story, politicians…Did the news story louse it up?* Having no information, George blanked. Silence. *Nothing further coming from Miss Walker? She's still not talking.* "How…how long will it be?"

"Three working days."

"Does it take three days to review the file?"

Silence again. George waited. *Nothing else? She's too polite to cut me off. She's waiting for me to give up and hang up.* Despite her obvious reticence, George tried to keep information coming. "Three days, Miss Walker?"

"Yes, I'll call you Tuesday and let you know."

Panicked, George thought, *Know what? Whether we get the child? Should I ask?*

Trembling, he tried to clear his throat. He didn't recognize his hoarse voice. "Let me know what, Miss Walker?"

Silence.

"We're...we're planning a welcome party for him, the evening of the thirtieth."

Silence, like a deep black hole opened up for him to whirl dizzily into. "Three...three days, Miss Walker?"

"Yes, I will call you Tuesday and let you know."

"You'll let us know?" *Stupid,* he castigated himself, *she just said that.* He obliged her by hanging up. He sat, gloomy, jerked around by forces he didn't understand. Fears rushed into his brain, dissolved it to useless mush.

Chapter 14

Bruce, the young legislative page, picked Jessica up in a state car at the airport and whisked her to the capitol. Jessica noted his impeccable appearance in dark bluejacket, tie and white shirt, his hair cut and combed flawlessly. Jessica smiled, almost giggled to herself. *Another 'every hair in place.' About Jonathon's age,* she guessed, *but on such different paths; Jonathon roiling against and escaping the establishment.*

In the capitol building, Bruce guided her to the door marked *Health and Human Services* and pulled it open. "The committee is waiting for you in here, Mrs. Keebler."

"Thank you."

Portly John McSweeny met her at the door. "Jessica Keebler?"

Jessica was jolted by the harsh rasp of his voice, but his tone was kindly. *Apparently some physical impairment.* "Yes," she answered, and let him shake her hand enthusiastically.

"John McSweeny," he said, "chairman of the Health and Human Services Committee. Thank you for coming, Mrs. Keebler."

"Thank you for inviting me, Mr. McSweeny."

He gestured her to the chair at the head table that faced a semicircle of seated men.

Jessica's antennae were extended and throbbing as she walked the ten feet to the indicated chair. The strong smell of cigar smoke smote her. *So male, so male.* She put her brief case on the table and lowered her purse to the floor beside her. Even before she sat and faced them she thought, *Not a dress in sight.*

Twelve lounging men looked curiously at her, some disinterested because their source of power had nothing to do with the adoption lady from Los Angeles. She could be of little consequence to them. Slouched comfortably in their authority, body bulges rumpled their suits, shirts and ties. One hand-held cigar was contributing its unhurried smoke signals to the male ambiance of the room accentuating Jessica's feeling that she'd walked into a private club, males only.

Jessica argued silently with what her senses were telling her, defending her professional world. *My work world is dresses, slacks, smart suits, cosmetic fragrances, and caring about babies. Smoking at the agency is confined to the restrooms, no sour stench in offices or meeting rooms, no crumpled male clothing.*

Taking her seat, Jessica felt the weakness of her lone femaleness under spotlighting stares of ruling males. Thirty two years in California's underfunded social work had layered over Jessica's intuitive caring with a veneer of cynicism about the political males who decided the sums of social work budgets. Now her senses of sight and smell affirmed the correctness of her attitude. *Yet these are the very ones I have to impress, nay, convince to allow this adoption.* Jessica broke off her indulging in the correctness of her opinions and thought about where to start in her presentation.

To help her resist the intimidation of their male-dominant presence, Jessica avoided looking directly at them. She slowly opened her brief case and took out the Liebman file including the complete history of the 'Lee' baby. She opened the folder and rearranged sheets as if organizing her notes for the presentation. She did it only to remind herself why she was there, to not let powerlessness destroy her focus. She touched the case records to emphasize to herself how comfortable she was directing biological, adoptive and foster parents, babies and staff for all of LA County. *I'm here, gentlemen, because I know more about these matters than you do.* She glanced at the man holding the cigar, who peacefully watched his contribution of drifting smoke. Seeing the smoke made the sour smell seem stronger. *Yes,* she reaffirmed, *I know more about babies than you men do.*

Beside her, McSweeny stood and gaveled twice to open the meeting. Jessica fingered the edges of the controversial Liebman file as she listened. "Gentlemen, Mrs. Keebler, director of the LA County Bureau of Adoptions, has been good enough to answer our urgent call for information concerning the change in the state's adoption guidelines proposed by Steve Gorelni, State Director of Adoptions."

Blessings on you, Steve, thought Jessica.

McSweeny continued. "Because we have to make a recommendation to the legislature today, we will dispense with the time-consuming question-and-answer formalities. I'll ask Mrs. Keebler to simply tell us what the situation is with the LA County Bureau of Adoptions." McSweeny turned to his guest. "Mrs. Keebler." McSweeny laid his gavel on the table and sat.

"Thank you, Mr. Chairman," Jessica said. She decided to speak from her chair, to make it an informal offering of information rather than a major presentation. She took a moment to plan silently. *Slowly, space it. Don't rush your points away. Make sure they get it before you go on.* Jessica inhaled, then let it out. "Gentlemen, we are faced with a crisis in the LA County Bureau of Adoptions." The familiar ring of her words recalled her meeting with her interns. *But here, I'm not authority telling them what will be. I'm supplicating. How to make them understand?*

"We are averaging an inflow of eleven babies a month released by birth mothers for adoption. A high percentage of these infants are inter-racial and, under the present law, must go to Negro homes. But Negroes have not been asking to adopt, creating the impasse in foster homes, and these babies are considered *unadoptable.*" Jessica stopped to think if she could provide more context that would help these men, so far removed the problems, to better understand. She added, "White families are adopting the White babies turned over to us, but very few families of color ask for the 'mixed,' the 'unadoptable' ones, the eighty percent. They are piling up in foster homes with more coming each day."

Jessica stopped for a deep breath. She quailed at the heavy burden of her task. *No tears, Jessica.* She compressed her lips. "We have eight-ty-sev-ven unadoptable children in foster homes. Some of them are already toddlers…a year-and-a-half…one is *two years old.* The paper work is being done to transfer the older ones to Child Welfare.

At two, however, this child doesn't yet know what a home is, what love is!" Jessica knew the stats for such a child were eventual suicide or a life of crime, but she feared she couldn't get into that without tears. She continued, "To relieve the mounting congestion, I am forced to ask for more staff." Again feeling the authority of her facts, Jessica scanned the men before her. "Will you increase my budget?" Jessica heard demanding anger in her voice. *Easy does it, Jessica. The facts talk for you.*

Thinking of her next words raised and dropped her hands in an appropriate gesture of inadequacy. "We've had to accept foster homes that are not up to standard. The *LA Times* made *that* situation known to all of California. Some White foster parents can't relate to a 'mixed' baby. We have not always been successful anticipating the racist attitudes of some applicants. Much of our time at staff meetings and case-work time in the field is devoted to educating, lessening the negative impact of…uh…unenlightened…foster parents." Jessica recalled Emily insisting that the 'Lee' baby be removed to a *third* foster home. Despite her resolution, tears of frustration blurred her focus. She raised the Liebman file for them to see. "Gentlemen," she said loudly to keep herself on track, "we have here the application of a White family that asked for a child of *any national origin.*"

Some faces showed surprise. "Yes," Jessica said, nodding to them, "I too, found it unusual, but with the thought of possibly relieving the baby congestion, we explored the feasibility." In the pause Jessica congratulated herself for finding the verbal balance between plausibility of a placement and defiance of the law. "In the processing we found that the members of this family engage in daily activities with many racial groups in positive ways. They are prepared to love and raise an interracial child."

Some of the men shifted their positions. The tall man with the cigar cleared his throat, *Very loudly,* Jessica thought.

"We have the opportunity, gentlemen, to give perhaps half of our unadoptable babies permanent, loving homes if the California law is changed." Tears blurred her focus again. Jessica blinked and shook her head. "You must know, gentlemen, how important it is for a child to feel that he or she *belongs in a family, feels loved* by that family." Jessica knew she was talking female talk to this all-male audience. *But they have to hear this. They have to be told how their laws are affecting the lives of others.*

Jessica thought she'd said enough. To sum up, she spoke slowly, pointedly, thinking to end in a few sentences. "The adult is the result of what the child experiences. Without love, we will have more negative citizens." Jessica tied her facts into the economics of social work. "Neglected, unloved children cost the state millions of dollars in welfare, juvenile and medical services, law enforcement and incarceration. Unloved children grow up to be angry, incorrigible opponents of the law, or depressed, passive wards of the state, either way they swell the state's budget. The adult *is* what the child has experienced. Our present position, denying children homes because of an accident of birth, is untenable from a humane point of view, or if only in light of the dollars and cents facts of business." Jessica silently replayed what she'd just said and decided it was enough. "Thank you, gentlemen."

There was a long silence. McSweeny looked at his committee members. "Any questions?"

Walter Jamison spoke. "Yes."

"You're recognized, Walter."

"Mrs. Keebler, have you chosen a baby for this family?"

"Yes, we have."

"What kind of baby have you chosen?"

"His mother is Chinese and his father is Negro."

Tom Shafron interrupted. "And a White family is accepting him?"

Roy Ambrose broke in pointedly. "A *Jewish* White family."

Jessica's head snapped to look at Ambrose. *The cigar smoker. Who informed him about the Liebmans?*

"Quite a mix," Shafron said.

Jessica thought she heard a snicker after his comment. Anger poured from her, burning like hot lava. "We chose this boy because he's one of our most desperate cases. We've had to remove him from *two* foster homes because the foster parents neglected him. To them he was a *nationality*, a *foreigner,* not a human being that needs to be loved. The present law treats mixed babies as foreign nationalities. These babies are American citizens, born in America, to be placed where they will be loved!" Her pulse racing, Jessica sat back and breathed deeply, then continued. "You've read about the foster home scandal in the *LA Times.* Yes, you were all shocked that it was happening in the prosperous state of California, but our budget has *not* been increased for more home inspection staff. Instead of paid professionals, to supervise the care of the babies, I'm operating with five volunteer interns doing their graduate field work with us. When they leave, we'll have to break in new graduate students. Our staffing situation is no better than when the scandal broke and our case load increases daily; not an exaggeration, gentlemen, *daily.*" Jessica's intensity had bent her forward again. She realized she was glaring at them. She exhaled abruptly and sat back. Relieved of some of her fury, she could again observe their faces. *They're listening. Anger works. It is not unprofessional to get angry.*

She spoke more quietly into the attentive silence. "Numbers," she said and let the word hang there for them to wrestle with. "No one expected teenage, inter-racial pregnancies to rise so dramatically, creating these unanticipated pressures." Jessica thought she'd said enough to leave it alone. *Wait for questions,* she told herself. The minimal opposition so far encouraged her. *Then again, details of the pending adoption might make a stronger case.*

Jessica cleared her throat and breathed deeply before launching the case history.

"The 'Lee' baby was released to a foster home immediately after birth, to a couple that supplemented its income with foster parent checks. They had done fairly well with a White baby previously. It was a week before the field worker returned to check the baby's progress. Giving me her report, she sat in my office and cried. The White foster parents could not deal with an inter-racial baby. Lee was removed to a second home. The tragedy was repeated. I made a note to change the foster parent application to ferret out racial prejudice. Yes, they'd attended the orientation session, said they understood their responsibilities and they'd raised three children of their own. However," Jessica let her anger rise to block her tears, "*however,*" she repeated, "at a time when an infant needs to be touched and held to develop his trust for adults, Lee lay neglected in his crib. Tested at four months, his neurological responses had slowed. He was semi-catatonic. He broke out in allergies. He had diarrhea. Do you know what neglect does to an infant? In that early stage when the brain is maturing?" Jessica paused, then slapped the table sharply, startling her audience. "Without love, gentlemen, the brain does not mature!" Jessica sat back, lifted her glasses and unselfconsciously dabbed at her eyes with a tissue. "Of course, we moved him to a third foster home…"

Jessica stopped because she was feeling drained. She ended quickly. "The 'Lee' boy is eight months old. All the necessary interviews and visits with the adoptive family have come up positive. The physical and neurological tests of the baby are completed. He is ready to be adopted."

She hoped she'd said enough and said it so they understood. Though near emotional exhaustion, she felt impelled to add, "For the sake of the children, I've changed my view of the state's policy of racial separation. I hope you will change yours." *Is it enough? What else to convince them?* She thought with grim humor, *I could sit here and cry to prove how desperate we are.*

Instead, Jessica leaned back, looked over their heads and whispered, "Gentlemen, you've got to let these children go to homes where they can be loved."

Jessica closed her eyes and breathed deeply. *So I end with a whimper.* She was startled by the isolated sound of one man clapping. Jessica looked at him with a tired, grateful smile. Two others joined the applause, then John McSweeny.

Jessica nodded and mouthed a soundless, "Thank you."

A silence followed. Jessica wondered whether there would be more questions. Her early morning flight had landed her in Sacramento at nine-five. She glanced at her watch. Ten-ten. Suddenly the emptied feeling inside her turned to hunger, but she had a negative reaction to staying for lunch. *I've had enough of being with men. I'll eat at Phil's and finish the day at the agency.*

McSweeny struggled his weight upward to a standing position and turned partly to address his guest. "You've certainly put it on the table for us, Mrs. Keebler. Thank you." He turned to the others. "Further questions, gentlemen?"

"Yes."

"You're recognized, Roy."

Roy Ambrose lay his lit cigar in the ash tray and for a moment watched the thin line of smoke trail upward. "Mrs. Keebler, I commend you for your concern for your wards, but are you aware of the civil strife that occurs from a mixing of the races?"

Anger revved Jessica back up to alert. "Of course," she snapped, "but this adoption is not arbitrary. It is a thoroughly screened process in which qualified, responsible adults are asking for a child to love, not hate."

Ambrose picked up his cigar and puffed it once. "I'm thinking of the larger picture, Mrs. Keebler, beyond the family. In mixed neighborhoods frictions develop. They can quickly go out of control. It's no longer a safe place to live. Real estate values drop. Local businesses fail. Much as I admire your concern for the babies under your supervision...Mr. Chairman, I think our recommendation to the legislature should be 'tabled for further study'."

"Is that a motion?"

"Yes."

McSweeny turned to the others. "Is there a second?"

Silence.

McSweeny continued to wait, then banged his gavel. "Without a second, the motion is lost." McSweeny turned to his guest. He noticeably softened his hoarse rasp of a voice. "Mrs. Keebler, I know you came here in response to our request for information and you've done it admirably. I'd like to make the rest of your stay more pleasant. I'll have the page show you some of the capital sights and you can join us for lunch before you fly back."

"Thank you, Mr. McSweeny, for your kind offer, but I do have to get back." Jessica put the Liebman file into her brief case as she continued talking. "I would appreciate a ride to the airport as soon as possible."

"Of course. Bruce is waiting to escort you. And again, thank you for taking the trouble and for your excellent presentation."

As Jessica stood up, McSweeny put down his gavel and applauded. This time the response from the others was stronger than before, with added 'Hear hears' and 'Thank you for coming.' Only Roy Ambrose did not applaud.

Jessica smiled gratefully, turned to the bank of men, nodded and said repeated 'Thank yous.' The applause floated Jessica to the door where McSweeeny stood holding it open. He shook hands with her enthusiastically. "Splendidly done. Thank you again."

Bruce stood up from his chair and waited for her. Jessica followed him to the elevator.

McSweeny released the door and returned to his chair at the table. Before he could continue the meeting, Ambrose spoke. "Gentlemen, we've got to proceed cautiously."

McSweeny flared. "Does your 'cautiously' mean not to proceed at all?"

"Do you realize that we are teetering on the edge of legislating the mixing of the races in California?"

"Wholly constitutional since that document reads, 'All men are created equal'."

"Yes, but it's never been done!"

McSweeny slammed the gavel on the table making his committee members jump. "So it's never been done. Isn't it about time? In 1856 no one ever heard of an automobile or an airplane, but we sure got them now. And I wish you'd stop smoking cigars in the committee room! You hear this voice? It's from smoke. I quit. I wish you would."

Ambrose crushed the lit end in the ash tray. "Don't change the subject, John, and don't cut off discussion. We haven't thought this through."

"That's a matter of opinion, Roy." McSweeny turned to the others. "How many of you are ready for the vote?"

Only five of the twelve hands went up.

McSweeny folded his arms over his chest. His words were bitter. "All right, if you're not ready for the vote we can have lunch brought in, and then, if you're still not ready for the vote, dinner."

Walter Jamison spoke up. "There are serious considerations, John, that we haven't addressed."

McSweeny raised both hands and bowed his head in mock honor to Jamison. "And what is your compromise, Daniel Webster?"

"This test adoption could open a floodgate, John." He added, "It undoubtedly will."

"And inundate us with what?"

"With the placements of these children regardless of race."

"And isn't that what the constitution guarantees?"

Jamison ignored that. Deep in concentration, he continued to pick his words carefully.

"It would be a legal recognition of..."

All twelve pairs of eyes were on Jamison, waiting.

Jamison repeated it more slowly. "It would be a legal recognition..."

McSweeny leaned forward in his chair. His harsh rasp intensified his impatient tone.

"Legal recognition of what, Walter?"

"That there is...no difference.... It could be interpreted that way..."

Ambrose jumped up. "It certainly could be interpreted that there is no differences in the races, Walter. And we know that's not true. Just look at the Blacks, the Mexicans, the Chinese. The differences are obvious. Your cautions are well founded, Walter."

Jamison frowned unhappily and turned to face Ambrose directly. "I do rethink my position when I find myself in agreement with you, Roy."

"Gentlemen," McSweeny said, "we have to give our recommendation to the legislature today. Walter, do you have a motion for the floor?"

All eyes turned to Jamison again.

"Let me say first, Mr. Chairman, that while I have no objection to a change in the state's adoption policies, if the Liebman case is allowed, there's no question it will become a precedent."

"No doubt, Walter," McSweeeny agreed, "and with good reason. Steve Gorelni made it clear. Not only Los Angeles, but San Francisco, Sacramento, San Diego — all have the same need; increasing numbers of babies in substandard foster homes." McSweeny turned to face Ambrose squarely. "Because our antiquated policy *segregates* babies from possible adoptive parents."

"Two years ago, Mr. Ambrose," McSweeny continued, "the Supreme Court declared segregated schools unconstitutional in the *Brown vs. Board of Education* decision." His hoarse voice dropped to a raspy whisper. "Hundreds of babies are lying segregated from possible adoptive parents while we are talking...you heard the woman...because California still believes in segregation. Why, gentlemen? This isn't Alabama or Mississippi." He stopped suddenly as with a new thought to scan all of them. "Or would you have the mixed babies legally declared 'unadoptable' and raise them in a state orphanage?" He scanned the committee with an intense stare. "This is beyond politics, gentlemen. Where is your humanity?"

Thomas Gladden spoke up. "I agree with you, John, and I'm sure most of us do, but I don't think our constituents are ready for this. Yes, what Mrs. Keebler is asking *is* constitutional. Even Roy Ambrose will have to accept that. But there's a lot of racial prejudice out there in the boonies."

McSweeny shot back. "Are you saying that racial prejudice is the mandate to this committee? We were elected to make decisions. Can we relinquish leadership to the boonies?"

"I do think we have to go slow, John," Gladden said.

Pushing for a vote, McSweeny scanned their faces, but saw the majority indecisive.

He called for the motion anyway.

No one spoke.

McSweeny threw up his hands and let them plop on the table in frustration. "So you're not ready for a vote." He picked up the gavel and banged it on the table. "Break for lunch."

Head spinning, Jessica extended her hand toward the flight attendant indicating that she wanted to be helped to mount the portable step up to the shuttle's opened door. He obligingly took her arm and steadied her into the cabin. Inside the small twin-prop plane, seats were not reserved. Jessica chose to sit at a window. Seeing only three other passengers, Jessica freed herself of her purse and brief case using the empty seat next to her. She parked her elbow on the narrow window ledge and dropped her head onto her hand. She massaged her temples, one with a thumb, the other with the fingers of the one hand. *I'm not used to this. I don't deal with men enough. They can't see what I see.*

The overhead sign beeped steadily. Jessica reached for the ends of her seat belt and fastened it. She pulled the adjustment belt until it was tight against her abdomen, holding, keeping her from falling apart. It felt good to be held. *We're so isolated from men in what we do.* She remembered that a man, Steve Gorelni was director of the State Adoptions office, recalled her subtly prodding him on the phone. *He did put it on their agenda. But he's up in the middle of the bottleneck of politics ... Will they even make a decision this afternoon?*

Jessica thought of Ambrose's patronizing question. *Do I know that mixing the races causes civil strife?* Jessica smiled weakly at her energy drain that could fuel only her annoyance at his intentional misrepresentation. *His kind of politician is a master of deceit for the status quo.* Too tired, Jessica closed her eyes, but couldn't resist a last internal shot at Ambrose, *Baby killer.*

But relaxation was not possible without first putting other thoughts to rest. *Steve knows we need a decision before Thursday to tell the Liebmans yes or no. I hope he stays on it. He did lay it out clearly for them. Nice to know he's still for the kids.*

What little energy Jessica generated by relaxing, she put to the immediate service of her anxious mind. *Did I do any good?* She couldn't resist a moment-by-moment review of her Health Committee grappling. Remembered high points bounced back and forth in her head, hoping to put to rest her uncertainty of, *Was it worth it?* She breathed deeply, trying to focus on something more useful. *Steve'll call and let me know their decision. Glad he's still on my side in this. He can't put nine years into Child Welfare and not want to do something for kids the rest of his life.* Jessica felt a sudden dizziness. Her eyes popped open but she still felt that she was swinging out of balance. *Not migrane, not vertigo, please, God.* She tensed down into her seat to fight it, to restore equilibrium, then realized it was the twin-engined shuttle swinging into the wind, pivoting to taxi out to the runway. The light plane fluttered like a butterfly. Relieved that it was the plane turning and not her, Jessica smiled gratefully and snuggled back into the comfort of her seat. Feeling safe again, Jessica smiled, enjoying the gentle rocking as it taxied toward takeoff. *Like mothers rock babies.* The sudden roar of the engines speeding toward takeoff frightened her again. The tires rumbled on the rough concrete, sending vibrations through plane and passengers. The plane lifted and vibrations ceased, and Jessica felt she was floating peacefully. She relaxed into her seat and closed her eyes. *I have to tell Roberta what happened, but I don't think I can face the office. I'll call her from my house. She can tell the others that there's nothing so far.* The brilliant sunshine seemed to stack sparkling jewels against the thick glass of her porthole of a window. Jessica smiled down at them. *If Steve calls tonight...I'll call Roberta at her house. Even if he doesn't call, I'll have to tell Roberta, 'nothing yet.' She has to be as anxious as I am.*

Before getting into bed, Jessica picked up the phone again, dialed and listened to it ring. "Roberta, Jessica again. I didn't wake you, did I?...Good. Steve hasn't called, apparently no decision yet. I'll see you in the office tomorrow...Thanks, you too. 'Bye."

Chapter 15

Wednesday morning Jessica sat at her desk. She had her hand on Emily's Baby Lee file but hadn't opened it. She fingered the stiff edge of the Manila cover, but didn't go any further. Annoyed at her inertia, she thought, *I don't have to read this again. I know it word for word. My decision is made and I've done what I can to make it happen.* Jessica released the file, raised her hands and dropped them. *I can no longer influence how it will go.*

Jessica put away Emily's file and pulled up Janice and Alicia's latest reports on their cases. She looked at the blank Manila but didn't open either one. Jessica glanced at her watch. Nine-forty. *Are you going to sit here all morning waiting for Steve's call? All day?*

Jessica remembered her impatience with the men in Sacramento ringed in front of her, so removed from understanding what the babies were going through. *How hard it was to make them understand. Did I succeed? Two days and nothing yet. I told the Liebmans they'd hear from me tomorrow. The committee could kill Steve's resolution. If so, the Liebmans will hear bad news.*

Failure suddenly washed over Jessica, making her feel sick, slumped her in her chair. She'd wasted her time, her energy, her tears in Sacramento. She dropped her glasses to let them hang and grabbed a tissue to her eyes. Angry at herself for breaking, she bounced up and went to the door, stood there with her hand on the knob with the thought of threatening to open it and let everyone in the well-trafficked corridor see what she was letting happen to her.

She dried her eyes, put her glasses on, walked out of her office to the switchboard. "Any messages, Nancy?"

Surprised, Nancy looked up. "Uh…no, Jessica."

"Thanks." Jessica went back, passed her office, went on to the restroom.

Walking helped. Back in her office she sat at her desk and opened Alicia's file.

Jessica made notes, thought of questions to ask Alicia. The morning dragged. By a quarter to twelve Jessica was hungrier than usual and decided to tackle Janice's file after lunch. *I'll go to Phil's early and beat the crowd. Maybe Roberta will join me.*

But Roberta didn't answer her phone. Jessica buzzed the switchboard.

"Yes, Jessica."

"Is Roberta in the building?"

"No. She's due back at one-thirty."

"Thanks."

Eating her salad, Jessica was hoping Evelyn the cashier would beckon wildly to her through the noise, holding the phone out to her with the other hand. But Evelyn was showing a group of four to a table. Jessica relaxed into the familiarity of the laughter and loud talk and became aware of the chef's good flavors in her sole almondine.

Driving back to the agency, it suddenly felt so routine to be heading to her office from Phil's. *I ought to do something exciting on my vacation.* The thought of trying to plan a vacation without Lenny stopped her. She grimaced against her sudden need to cry. *It takes so long, so long.* Remembering his pain in his last months, she was suddenly no longer angry at him for leaving her. He didn't want to leave. He didn't want to leave. *Lenny, Lenny.*

Forgiving him didn't make it any easier for her to think of vacation alone. *Another year of planning a vacation without Lenny.* Jessica was surprised, and relieved, that it wasn't hurting so much.

She rolled her window down to smell fresh air. She breathed deeply. The bright March sunshine had become routine too. She had a sudden impulse to drive to San Pedro, watch the fishing boats and smell the Pacific salt water. Jessica smiled wanly as she parked at the agency and shut off the ignition.

In the building she stopped at Nancy's for messages. There were none. "Roberta back?"

Nancy shook her head. "One-thirty."

In her office Jessica sat, wondered what Steve's message would be…when he might call.

Dully she reached down to her staff actives, put Janice's file on her desk and sat.

She turned her notepad to a fresh page, put her pen on the pad and sat. Dull, yes, but no longer in the agitating grip of anxiety, anger or eagerness. Somewhere deep inside she was pretending she didn't care anymore. *If I have to, I'll continue with our bumbling, fumbling efforts to cope with the improbabilities those men have burdened us with. If they don't have the brains, the humanity…What a fool I was to use the word 'love' to them. So foreign to their politics. They don't even know how to spell it.*

Jessica exhaled sharply as if she were ridding herself of that committee room, her anxieties there, her time, talking, pleading…*I offered them thirty-two years of experience. What a waste. What a waste.* Jessica began to worry about the negative effects her pessimism was having on her. *Self-preservation, Jessica, self-preservation.*

A ring of the phone startled her. "Oh-h!" she cried out as if she'd been hit.

Shaking, she picked up the phone, dropped it on her desk, grabbed it with two hands. "Yes?"

"Anything yet, Jessica?"

"Oh, Roberta…No, not yet. Not yet."

"As soon as you hear…"

"Of course, of course, as soon as I hear. You'll be the first."

"Thank you, Jessica. I *am* anxious."

"Of course, dear." Jessica cradled the phone, grateful that Roberta had called. "Well, there's two of us." *Nice not to be alone. Nice not to be alone.* Jessica readied her pad and pen and opened Janice's file.

Chapter 16

Monday morning, George woke as tense as when he went to bed. The tightness in his head was unrelieved by the thrashing that had consumed his sleep time. *Damn!* he thought, *another whole day before we know.* He heard Amy pad down the short hall to the bathroom and close the door. He lay there until he heard her leave the bathroom, then slipped out of bed, carefully, so as not to wake Lil. He went to the bathroom, showered and put on his house slacks and shirt.

When he came out, Amy was sitting at the table slicing a banana into her *Wheaties*. Lil was still asleep in their divan/bed at the far end of room, so neither George nor Amy talked.

Amy got up to get the milk.

George put on the kettle and took out a tea bag.

Amy poured milk on her cereal, sat down and sipped at her orange juice.

George brought his mug of tea to the table and sat opposite Amy. They sipped silently.

"I'm up," Lil said, and continued to lie quietly in bed.

"How do you like your new room, Amy?" George asked.

About to put a full spoon into her mouth, Amy changed course and returned it to the bowl.

"How many times are you gonna ask me that, Pops? It's great. I love it."

George smiled sheepishly. He didn't mind her annoyance. Today, caught in the tension of waiting yet another day for the agency's call, he needed to feel some success for all his hard work. "Good. I think Hank's plans worked out fine."

"Yeah," Amy answered.

"This damn business of waiting," George continued, "reminds me of the opening chapter in Steinbeck's *Tortilla Flat.*"

141

George's expression, 'damn business of waiting,' caught Lil's attention as well as Amy's.

She listened to George go on as she lay in bed, instead of planning her Thursday classes.

"He writes about the young male gopher," George narrated, "who's mature and ready to mate. He leaves his mom, comes to the flats to set up house and attract a partner. He picks a spot hidden in tall weeds and starts digging. Pretty soon he's got the long main run dug out, a couple of side runs, an escape run if all the others get blocked, and a special room for a nursery. When he's got it all built, he shakes himself clean, grooms his fur until it shines, and sits outside the entrance, hoping some young miss gopher will think he's too handsome to leave sitting there all by his lonesome. But no lady gopher shows."

Amy stopped eating and was listening.

"He sits next to the beautiful house he's built," George went on, "and waits, and waits." George fingered the handle of his mug. "That's just about where we are."

"Yeah," Lil said. "It's a pain." She swung the covers back and padded to the bathroom in her pajamas.

"That seems to be the theme of the book," George continued. "All the men who live in the shacks on the flat, seem to be waiting for something to happen." George returned abruptly to reality. "Wanna ride, Amy?"

"A ride?"

"To school."

"Sure. How come?"

"I'll go in early for my morning class and work on choreography. Beats this waiting here."

"Sure, waiting for the bus is a pain."

"Twenty minutes? I'll take a quick breakfast."

"I'll be ready."

Lil returned from the bathroom. She opened the casement window in the wall at the foot of the bed and welcomed the fresh morning air. She shook out the covers and straightened them over the bed and arranged the large and small cushions.

"What are you gonna do, Lil?" George asked.

"Stay home and work on lesson plans."

George dropped Amy off at school and went on to *Dance Center*. Closing the front door behind him, he walked through the office, glad that Theresa would not be in until ten, when his class would begin, and went into the studio. The large, silent, empty space welcomed him into its waiting conspiracy of total privacy. *Delicious*, thought George. Holding his dance bag, George stood, listening to the silence. He smiled. The silence was cleansed of any concern on the street beyond the closed front door. He bent and slid his bag to the side. He extended his arms into the silence above and stood still, felt the cells of his stretched skin along the sides of his body wake.

To exclude even the studio space from his awareness of himself, George closed his eyes, and breathed out to expel stimuli from his internals. Without plan of mood or story, without thought of rhythm or melody, he moved slowly. Without vision, without sound, his slow movement carried him away from any thought that tried to engage him. Deprived of sense stimuli, his slow movements went unrecorded, to be left where they took him, forgotten as he moved on with no purpose other than the aliveness of moving.

At some point he stopped, knew that his knees were bent, his body balanced to one side. He straightened, opened his eyes and stood for a moment, smiling. He looked for his bag, picked it up, and went into the dressing room to change into leotard and tights.

He heard Theresa's key in the front door. She called to him from the office entrance to the studio. She'd seen his car parked at the curb.

"Out in a minute," he answered.

When he joined her in the office, she showed him a letter from the IRS. "They're asking for a documented statement proving that we deserve our tax-exempt, 501 C 3 status as an educational institution."

"After seven years of being a community, non-profit corporation?"

"They want a detailed description of our activities."

"If they don't get us one way, they'll try another."

"Can we prove that we are, George?" Her voice was anxious. Theresa was as devoted to *Dance Center* as George and Lil. For her small salary and a scholarship for her daughter Dee, she kept the files, sent out the bills, dealt with the parents, had tickets printed for the concerts and did whatever other white collar chores came up. Thinking of proving their right to exist to the IRS, she offered, "I get the big okay from the parents when they're sitting here, about how much we're doing for their kids. With our classes, performances and family folk dance nights, they think we're doing a great job in the community. "Can we document it?"

George frowned, unwilling to get into it before teaching. "I'll have to. Can it wait until after I know which way the adoption goes?"

"We have sixty days."

George handed the letter back to her. He'd barely scanned it. "Show it to me again next week. I'll take care of it."

"Okay. What happened with *your* audit?"

"They dropped it. Even *they* knew their claim was ridiculous."

"Now this," Theresa said. "Is it doable?"

George nodded instantly. "Sure." George heard Paul's warm-up runs on the piano in the studio. He looked at his watch. Ten. George was back in his real world. He turned and went into the studio, where his students were waiting.

Teaching, his voice sounded strange to him because it tensed upward in pitch. He demonstrated movements more than usual so he'd keep moving with the class. Moving with them, he felt in touch; he wasn't alone, and, proving that his body was capable of coordinated action, helped him feel sane.

Driving home for lunch, he wondered if there'd be a phone call. Then he reminded himself that Miss Walker had said she'd call on *Tuesday* and this was still Monday.

He made a tuna fish sandwich and sat down to eat. Just outside the window the work waited for him on the deck. He didn't have to teach until three-thirty. *Maybe I could put in a couple of hours before going to the studio? No, if I'm not focused, I'll make mistakes.*

George shook his head. He resigned himself to being concerned with nothing else but whether the agency's answer to the adoption would be 'yes' or 'no.'

The adoption process had been zipping along on four wheels until the right front tire blew, landing everyone in a ditch. Reporter Martin Peters suggested that John Birchers had scattered nails on the road. *Is that why Mrs. Keebler had to review our file, because Birchers oppose mixing the races?* George shook his head. *Condemning an infant to never know the love of a family is the meanest of hatreds.*

George felt powerless against unseen forces blocking one of the most important happenings of his life. *Is Keebler on our side in this? Of course, stupid, she's been moving it right along.* George could only shake his head in frustration.

Dry clumps of sandwich were sticking to the roof of his mouth. He got up and poured himself a glass of milk. He ate because it was lunch time. The food had no taste, but he didn't want to get hungry during the two-and-half hour teaching stretch. *Don't waste time trying to figure the Birchers, George. Furthering children, poor children, is not their thing.*

George's fear of losing the baby, erupted again. His mouth dried. The thought of swallowing the goo in his mouth made his stomach close up shop and post a sign saying, *Unh-unh, not here you don't.* George thinned the stuff in his mouth with a sip of milk and carefully swallowed it bit by bit. Only a smidgeon separated his fear of 'losing the baby' from his hated feeling of 'another failure.'

George put the sandwich down and bounced up to look out the window at the cul-de-sac below. The newly asphalted road looked sleek and black. George smiled. He remembered the days of walking up the long cement staircase with heavy shopping bags; in '48-'49, carrying the huge block of ice on his shoulder up to their ancient ice-box, before they bought the secondhand fridge.

Again he looked out and admired the curving road that opened passage right up to the house. *Quick access, big improvement. Big improvement. At least some things are working. And the bedrooms are finished. Amy's loving her new room.*

But his anxiety dragged him back to the Birchers. George remembered that they were thought to be a core of wealthy elite that successfully kept themselves screened from inspection, yet periodically shook up life in California. They influenced legislators to sponsor state loyalty oaths, outlaw the closed shop and coalesce racial ignorance to condemn hundreds of babies to lives without love. *Are the Birchers asking, 'Who is this Liebman family, swinging a sledgehammer on the status quo? And obviously Jews.'*

Standing, looking at it, the new road took on a different meaning. *Would they seek out the parking pocket that is Ewing Street and drive right up to the Liebman house on the new road? How dirty will they play to keep orphaned babies in captivity?*

George shook his head. "Dammit!" he hissed. *It's only two years after the Supreme Court's* Brown vs. Board of Education *decision that made segregation unconstitutional. The Court reminded the country, north and south, California to New York, territories Puerto Rico, Hawaii, Alaska, Guam, Samoa and any other US land areas, that all American children are to be treated equally.*

Pacing back to the table, he was too agitated to finish the sandwich. He put the rest of it in the fridge. *This adoption would rub the noses of the Birchers in Brown vs. Board of Ed. Syllable by syllable. How much opposition will the Birchers exert?*

Washing the glass in the sink, George imagined the far-right crazies howling at the Bureau of Adoption's projected move, *"You're destroying American values by polluting the White race!"*

Drying his hands, George recalled the baby Lee's face, thin, neglected, confused, hyper sensitive. George shook his head. *Do they know how cruel they are to this child?*

In danger of unnerving himself before teaching, George decided to go to the studio early. Better to talk with Theresa at the office and prepare to teach than sit at home and take a beating from the unseen monster. Walking down the three steps to the car right outside the new deck, he was choreographing new movements to the folk song,

Donkey Riding for the eight-year olds. Productive again, he felt alive despite his crisis.

Driving home, George felt pleased that he'd done well with both classes, but suddenly he tensed. *The call, the call.* He shook his head angrily. *Shmo! It's still Monday, tonight, all night, until tomorrow!*

Chapter 17

Monday afternoon, Jessica sat staring at Janice's file. She couldn't remember how many times she'd opened it without reading and noting the entries Janice had made of her last week's case-load activities. Twice Jessica had put the file back in the drawer, then taken it out again.

The afternoon had passed with Jessica frittering away the time finding things to do other than sitting in her office. She'd manufactured a conference with Roberta, then talked with Nancy to clarify some points of switchboard communications to staff. She looked at her watch. After attempting to check caseload files, the imminence of the five o'clock quitting time made her fearful that no decision will have been made until Tuesday. At five minutes to five, still hoping for the word, she called Roberta and then Nancy, asking them to stay until six. They agreed. Roberta felt, like Jessica, the call was the most important thing that could happen to her.

Jessica looked at her watch. Ten to six. She thought of giving up and going home. She looked at the silent phone. *I'll give it the ten minutes.* Jessica was glad that she'd asked Roberta and Nancy to stay on with her. Jessica didn't want to be alone in the empty agency building to receive the news no matter which way the Sacramento decision went.

Jessica was suddenly depressed to realize that her thoughts were almost wholly taken up with her abruptly depressed attitude she felt toward the work of the agency. The burden of the policy change she was attempting had made her unbearably vulnerable. She dreaded the thought of being asked to resign. Having committed an illegal procedure, she'd have no recourse to an appeal. Her fears of the risks she'd taken tightened her tensions, causing her to breathe shallowly, worry about her job, the future of the agency, with and without her, and the level of her blood pressure.

To turn off her anxieties she switched on an internal modus operandi that she'd learned as a girl on the elementary school playground. In the fourth grade when she wasn't chosen to be in the recess games, she'd pretended to herself, *I don't care about being in your games.* Not the truth, but it did cover over and dull her pain of being excluded.

Growing up, Jessica utilized this internal mechanism whenever there was danger of rejection. It maintained a facade of self-worth that kept her functioning until she latched on to other satisfactions.

Dully staring at Janice's opened file again, Jessica realized that the 'I don't care' mechanism had kicked in automatically to sustain her in case the Sacramento vote went against her. Janice's typed words and phrases, carefully chosen to make clear to Jessica the situation with each of her infants, held no interest for Jessica. She smiled. *I'm telling the agency and Roy Ambrose in Sacramento, you can't hurt me because I don't care.*

Lenny's exit from her life had also increased Jessica's vulnerability. Her tolerance for risk had been much greater when discussion with Lenny had helped clarify her options in a situation. Even if she chose to act wrongly and the decision went against her, empathetic Lenny had been there to catch her falling spirit. Jessica smiled thinly. *Self-preservation, Jessica, self-preservation, if Sacramento's answer is 'no.' Jessica Keebler still has to go on.* Jessica nodded in approval of her internal decision. As she'd decided so many times in the last four years, *Yes, Jessica Keebler has to go on, even without Lenny.*

Jessica felt more at ease with herself now that she better understood the reason for her abrupt disinterest in her daily tasks, and, equally, whether Sacramento agreed or disagreed with her stance. Having told the legislative committee what she believed should be done, and ratcheted up her every one of her cell's energy for her presentation, she'd at least built her own self-respect to buffer her against their *no*, even against their possible request for her resignation.

Jessica closed Janice's file. Bending to put it in the drawer, she thought, *They can't fire me from my convictions. They're the ignorant ones. I know what it takes for this agency to keep doing its job. If I give up what thirty-two years have taught me, I am nothing.*

Jessica closed the drawer. Deciding to totally close down her anxieties for the day and go home, she picked up the phone to call Nancy.

"Yes, Jessica."

"Thanks for staying until six tonight."

"You're welcome, Jessica."

"Find a time when you can come in late and make up for it."

"Thanks, I will."

Jessica cradled the phone, stretched, closed her eyes and breathed deeply.

The ring of the phone startled her. She picked it up.

"Steve Gorelni's on the line."

The strength went out of Jessica's hands. She fumbled the phone from one hand to the other, then dropped it. "Oh," she gasped, grabbing it hard. *Roberta, Roberta,* she thought, *I must talk to Roberta first.*

"Jessica, are you there?

But there's no time. "…Uh…yes, yes, Nancy…"

"Shall I put him through?"

"Yes, yes…of course, Nancy." Jessica heard the click. "St-Steve?" she whispered. She heard Nancy's "Go ahead, Mr. Gorelni."

"Jessica! You did it, Jessica! Congratulations!"

"They…they agreed?"

"Yes, they agreed. It wasn't easy. McSweeny stayed with it…"

Jessica couldn't hear the details of Steve's continuing report that rushed past like a flooding river, for the roaring in her head. Periodically she whispered her disbelief into his excited narration. "They….they agreed?" she breathed, sampling his unexpected 'yes', trying to understand it. She sampled it again. "They agreed…"

"Yes! Yes!" Steve affirmed, and his words tumbled fast and high-pitched. They bounced on the rapids of his excitement.

Finally, he was silent. Enthusiasm still bubbling about being part of history-being made, Steve summed it up. "Jessica, you've changed the course of adoptions in California. Congratulations!"

Jessica had pains in her head. Trying to talk was difficult. "Thanks, thanks," she whispered, "when...when can it happen?"

"As soon as your process is complete. Is it?"

"...Uh...yes, yes, it is. I'll...I'll tell Roberta."

"It's already on the radio up here. You're going to be swamped with requests!"

The roaring flooded back into her head. She barely managed, "That...that'll be good, Steve...good...thanks, Steve...'Bye." Jessica held on until she buzzed Roberta. "Yes... Roberta, yes," and sobbed loudly into the phone before putting it down.

Jessica, sounding like she'd had an attack, frightened Roberta. Hurrying, she didn't wait for an invitation to open Jessica's door. She was shocked to find Jessica crumpled in her chair, head almost on her knees, sobbing piteously. "Jessica! Jessica! Are you hurt?"

Jessica raised her head a bit to try to answer despite being wracked by sobs. "No...I...I'm fu...fine." Feeling shame for disintegrating before one of her staff, Jessica attempted to sit up, but her release from tension was so great, the sobs wracked her uncontrollably, tears poured. She fell back against the chair, helpless to stop her weeping.

Roberta pulled tissues and gave them to Jessica.

Unable to talk, Jessica let her glasses hang, held the tissues to her eyes. "I...I...don't know..."

"Don't try to talk, Jessica."

When the sobs quieted, Jessica tried to smile, but it distorted to a grimace. "We...we won...Roberta."

Roberta was surprised, and grateful, to be included in the victory. She felt an inner warming toward Jessica that broke through her constant awareness of their professional stations.

"Whu...what a way tu...to celebrate." Tears still rolling slowly from her eyes, Jessica looked up at Roberta. With a wry smile, she reached an arm toward Roberta.

Roberta saw a hurt child asking for help. She reached to take it.

Jessica raised her other hand.

Roberta didn't hesitate as Jessica stood to be embraced. Jessica, in her exhaustion, leaned against Roberta. Without thinking, Roberta accepted her. Her hands felt the moist warmth of her back, and of her head, cradled against her shoulder. She was grateful that Jessica included her in her victory. The feeling of being part of someone's joy she felt for the first time. Warmth expanded, flowed through her whole body. Holding Jessica, she realized she had never felt such physical joy. She swayed with Jessica, as if taking the tears from her in a slow dance. Her own eyes filled. They welled and rolled down Roberta's cheeks. She let them.

Chapter 18

Tuesday morning, with the sun's first light, George slipped out of bed, quietly so as not to wake Lil. He exchanged his pajamas for house clothes on the chair, and tiptoed into the kitchen to put them on. While setting water to boil for his herb tea and honey, he kept glancing into the living room waiting for the phone to ring, though he knew it was too early for Miss Walker to be at her desk.

Amy came in and George sat with her while she ate breakfast. He spoke in a low voice so as not to wake Lil. "Did you get your homework done?"

"Yes." Amy frowned, puzzled. "Have you changed over to an early morning person?"

"Miss Walker said she'd call today."

"It's only seven-thirty."

"I know. I'm on edge. I couldn't sleep." George watched Amy eat her cold cereal.

"Do you still want us to get the baby?"

Amy swallowed and looked at him. "Of course."

"It may or may not happen." As soon as it was out of his mouth, he was sorry he'd said it. *No sense burdening her day with something she can't do anything about.* George got up quietly. "Well," he mumbled, "we'll know when we get the phone call."

After Amy left, George thought of going back to bed, but that would surely wake Lil. *I don't need another unpleasantness.* He went out the back door into the still, quiet morning. In the sweet, cool air the young fruit trees sported green leaves to replace immature dried blossoms. Down the stone steps to the cellar, he filled one bowl with chicken feed, another with rabbit feed and walked the bumpy dirt trail at the bottom of the terraced hillside to the cages. He spread the chicken feed in the wooden trough for the hens and put the whole bowl of feed in the mother rabbit's cage because she was nursing a litter of five. Back to the cellar, he filled a smaller bowl for the buck. Beside the bottom step, George stopped at the young banana tree. A second frond was uncurling upward from inside the stem. He admired the strong green color and its courage, daring to push its way into the turbulent world.. He turned to admire the young trunks of the fruit trees on the three terraced rows above him, how they dressed the parched desert tan of the hillside with hope. Pleased, he smiled. *A few dollars and my labor make the difference.* Summing up his backyard assets, he looked at the chickens again, which reminded him to look for eggs.

There were three. George smiled. *Cash flow.* He carried them carefully up the stone steps.

In the house the phone was silent. The clock read eight-forty-five. George decided to shower. In the bathroom he dropped his clothes and stepped one foot into the tub. The phone rang. Startled, he whirled, but, one foot in the tub and one on the floor, he lost his balance and fell backward against the towel rack on the wall, which kept him upright. He grabbed for his bathrobe. The phone rang again. He ran, one hand in a sleeve, the robe, dragging.

He picked up the phone. "Hello?"

"Mr. Liebman?"

"Yes."

"You and Mrs. Liebman can pick up the baby Thursday morning at eleven."

Adrenaline shot up to his brain. He couldn't find words. Lil was scheduled to be teaching then. "Could you…they…change to — no, no, I'll…we'll get a substitute. Thank you, Miss Walker. Yes. Thursday morning at eleven will be fine. Thank you. Thank you."

"See you then, Mr. Liebman."

"Yes. Thank you."

George cradled the phone and started to call Lil, but she was up with the phone's ring and coming toward him. "It's a yes, Lil, a yes." She let out a "Yay!" and asked, "When? When can we pick him up?"

"Thursday morning at eleven. We'll get a substitute for your class.

Amy will have the day off from school."

"I'll call Jeannette and Helen and tell them it's a 'go' for the party."

From Tuesday on, George's head reverberated with *We're getting the baby. We're getting the baby.* Only teaching could interrupt the refrain. As usual, he stood silently in front of the class for a moment before beginning to focus everyone's attention to the slow stretches. Paul Schoop at the piano hit the introductory chord and George led his eighteen students into the easy swing and stretch series. *We're getting the baby. We're getting the baby* bubbled up into his mind, the words fitting themselves into the sweeping waltz rhythm of the piano.

Three minutes into the class, George was grinning so, he could hardly talk to explain the next movements. Even as he shared the exhilaration and joy of movement with his students, he had to share the extraordinary news with them. He flung his arms wide, interrupting the movement sequence. "Class, we're getting the baby!"

The quiet focus ended. There was an immediate cheer from the students. The studio filled with "When?" "When will it happen?" "How wonderful!" "Congratulations!"

It was minutes before the news was absorbed and the students quieted enough to again focus on their creative ritual of stretching and strengthening muscles. *I had to tell them,* was George's excuse to himself. He smiled through the rest of class.

Thursday morning Roberta knocked on Jessica's door.

"Come in, Roberta."

"How are you feeling, Jessica?"

"Fine. Excited."

"I am, too." Roberta sat in the chair alongside the desk. She smiled to Jessica. "It's an important day."

Jessica nodded. "I'm expecting a rush of requests when this gets out."

"I'll welcome the shift from foster home problems to more placement interviews."

In the pause, Jessica sat back in her chair, smiling easily. She felt pleased at the new comfort between them.

Roberta looked down at her hands, then at Jessica. "I really came here to ask you to join Emily and me when we hand over the baby to the Liebmans."

Jessica looked thoughtful, shook her head minutely and smiled sadly. "No, Roberta..."

"You're the one responsible for what's happening today."

"I've thought about it." She looked into Roberta's eyes, shook her head. "I don't think I could handle it emotionally." Her hand made a slow swiping gesture. "Enough with the tears."

Roberta smiled, nodded her understanding and asked, "You'll attend the agency event we're catering for you a week from tomorrow?"

Jessica nodded. "Yes, I should be healed by then." She looked at her watch. "It's a quarter-to-eleven. You and Emily should get going."

Roberta stood, straightened the pale blue jacket of her suit. Her face lit up with excitement. She tossed her head a bit. "It feels good to be making history. Social workers don't usually get noticed."

Jessica stood. Her hands raised slightly toward Roberta. "May I thank you for putting me back together?" She stepped forward.

Roberta lifted her hands and stepped into the embrace.

"Thank you, Roberta. Forgive me...for being the huggy type."

"Not...not at all, Jessica." Roberta squeezed awkwardly, learning to equal Jessica's enthusiasm.

On that Thursday morning in March, 1956, Lil, Amy and George Liebman started up the agency steps. George was so focused on his inner excitement that he had no thought of it affecting anyone else's existence but that of his own family. There was a scattering of people on the steps, but then the Liebmans weren't the only ones who had business with the agency.

The excitement of the day's eleven o'clock moment swept up George's pessimistic, cynical observations about the four-day postponement, wrapped them tightly and dropped them into some inner trash receptacle that George happily labeled, *Forget it.* This sac of disappointments lay next to his other wounding experiences that caused his scars of cynicism about life in America. The healing of getting the baby, and because getting the baby would dissolve one thin sliver of the racial barrier, warmed him, energized his muscles, made his body want to dance. He was high, floating up the steps with, *We win so much with this!*

Inside the agency, George spoke to the receptionist, then stood with Lil and Amy in the lobby, waiting.

Miss Walker and Miss Karelin carrying the baby, came out and walked together toward the waiting Liebmans. George, a practiced observer of *The body tells what the person is feeling*, saw their steps assume the solemn rhythm of a life-defining ritual. He, Lil and Amy, receivers of a life, filled to the full, stood waiting.

As the distance between the givers and the receivers lessened, all shared small, difficult smiles and glistening eyes. Forming a small circle, the procession stopped, all focused on the baby in Miss Karelin's arms. He was tense but quiet, as if he, too, honored the solemnity. After another moment of accepting silence, there was nothing else but to begin. Slowly, her eyes watering, Miss Karelin lifted the baby toward George. George reached and accepted him. Lil's and Amy's visions followed him into George's arms, and felt that they, as well, received him.

Tensing her lips to hold back tears, Miss Walker offered Lil a closed brown paper bag.

Her voice was hardly audible. "There are…three of his favorite toys…in here," she said, "and a warm bottle of formula for the ride home."

Lil accepted the bag.

Miss Walker showed Lil two sheets of paper. "This list…"

Lil turned the paper bag over to Amy and focused on the list with Miss Walker.

"On these two pages, we've listed the foods he's allergic to…" She stopped to clear her throat, then swallowed noticeably. "And…and the symptoms they cause."

George thought, *They didn't tell us he had allergies.*

Lil nodded, folded the pages and held them. She shook hands with Miss Walker.

"Thank you for all your help."

Amy reached her hand to shake with Miss Walker. "Thank you," Amy whispered.

Not daring words, Miss Walker acknowledged Amy's offering with a nod and wry smile. Amy repeated the sub-ceremony with Miss Karelin.

The rituals done, it was time. The five stood another moment, two tearful with loss, three, with joy. The drama on the faces of the social workers told George that this was *more* than a momentous moment for the Liebmans. *They're in pain. Turning him over to us...giving him up is more than just part of their agency job. It's like losing a child.*

Illustrated before him was the phenomena of child-adult bonding, something George had never experienced. He knew the word as it applied to strengthening of metals in war production, but he didn't know the word as it applied to parent and child. In dance, unless he moved with total passion of every cell, bonded with his choreography, the performance was not successful; a total amalgam of mind, body and spirit he sweated to achieve through repeated rehearsals. From his passion in dance, he recognized their bonding.

Seeing their deep loss, George had a new respect for the agency. *There was heart here. A government agency that turned out to be on my side.* For the moment he was not a contrarian. A rush of feelings created tumult, filled his eyes and shook his head slowly in wonder at the moment.

The weight in his arms reminded him that he was charged with getting this baby safely down the steps into the car and home. He took a last look at Misses Walker and Karelin to say goodbye. They didn't hear him. Their eyes were saying their last goodbyes to the baby, the eye of the hurricane that overwhelmed them all.

George's walk to the front doors was a mix of joy, triumph and wonder. It vindicated so much of his life, he felt light and light-headed. Amy held the heavy glass door open for him. George carefully crossed the threshold and stepped into LA's prettiest sunshine. The air smelled sweet.

The Liebmans paid no attention to people on the steps moving toward them.

George had one foot down the first step when he realized their voices were directed to him.

"Will you hold it there please."

"Can we see all three of you."

"Stand in a line please."

"Hold the baby higher, Mr. Liebman."

George thought, *He knows my name?*

Camera clicks and bulb flashes punctuated the instructing voices.

Unprepared for this encounter, George smiled awkwardly.

None of the reporters asked for an interview. Explanations ran through George's mind, his sudden mental clarity an epiphany. *Like Martin Peters, they've written their stories. Garnered from political fallout in Sacramento and locally from someone in the LA Bureau of Adoptions. Their newsrooms are only waiting for a photo of the event to illustrate their type.*

The Liebmans obliged by standing in a line so all three and the baby were clearly visible. The line of flashing cameras moved up slowly as the photographers tried for tighter and tighter shots. Then suddenly the press broke ranks, scattered and were gone, ever-running to be first.

It was a relief to be left alone. The Liebmans walked the long ramp of steps in a careful, even rhythm until they felt the solid sidewalk under their feet. They turned toward their car.

Lil slid into the back seat and George gave her the baby. Amy went around to get in next to her and hold the bottled formula at the ready in case the baby cried. George closed the door, tested it for security and hurried around to the driver's side.

Through the stop-and-start downtown traffic, George drove defensively, thinking, *Careful, careful, so much at stake, so much at stake*...up Sunset Boulevard to Echo Park Avenue, to Lakeshore, to Ewing Street.

He no longer had to park below in the cul-de-sac. Proudly George pulled onto the sleek, black driveway where there was now no danger of slipping on loose gravel. He'd provided a smooth ascent for bringing the baby home. He parked next to the six new steps up to the new deck, leading to the new side entrance.

The car at rest, a smell of feces smote them. George hurried the baby into the house.

Lil changed the first diaper. Amy assisted with the warm washcloth. George watched, preparing himself for when it would be his turn.

The baby cleaned, Amy carried him into the kitchen, sat and gave him the still-warm bottle from the brown paper bag. The baby taken care of, Lil and George prepared lunch.

"Mom, he finished only half of it," Amy said.

"Don't force him. Burp him. He always has to be burped after he eats."

After lunch, the phone rang. George answered. It was Jeannette. "George, you're in the paper! On the front page!" She could hardly talk. "Get…get the afternoon paper, George," she managed, "get the paper!"

As soon as George told Lil, she and Amy were out the door and into the car.

They came home with three copies of the afternoon *Times*. The editor gave it the left half of the front page.

COUNTY GIVES 'MIXED'
BABY TO WHITE FAMILY

In a history-shattering precedent, the Los Angeles County Bureau of Adoptions gave a baby of mixed racial background to the Caucasian family of Mr. and Mrs. Liebman.

The article went on for half the page length, but Lil skipped to the photograph to read the caption:

Mr. And Mrs. George Liebman and daughter, Amy, leaving the LA County Bureau of Adoptions with their racially-mixed son.

Dinner for the Liebmans that night was what anyone found in the fridge. At one minute before the six o'clock network newscast out of New York, George held the microphone of a tape recorder in front of the radio. Lil, holding the baby, was sitting at the table. She forked a mouthful of food for herself, put the fork down, picked up the bottle and held it for the baby. Amy sat facing Lil, alternately chewing and listening for the newscast.

The majestic fanfare for the evening news startled everyone to attention. "NBC's evening news." The chewing stopped. George started the tape, but the first item was the voice of Secretary of State Dulles warning us that we must win the cold war in the undeveloped countries of the world. George stopped the tape. "I don't need to preserve that for posterity."

A commercial came on. At the end of it, George tensed for a news item, but another commercial started. At the end of it, George's fingers hovered over the 'on' and 'record' buttons, but a third commercial came on. "There can't be more than three commercials," he muttered angrily. He poised his fingers. The newscaster announced that Pakistan had elected the first Islamic government in the world. *"...It means,"* the speaker emphasized, *"that only a practicing Muslim can be President."*

George relaxed and took a breath. Lil and Amy were chewing again. The baby was sucking contentedly. The newscaster began. *"In Los Angeles today..."* George pressed the buttons. The chewing stopped. *"...County Bureau of Adoptions, in a precedent-shattering move, gave a racially-mixed baby to the Caucasian family of Mr. and Mrs. Liebman. This change in the guidelines for state adoptions in California was prompted by the record backlog of babies in foster homes, which is draining the resources of the state's health and welfare budgets."* The radio went to commercial.

George hit the stop button on the tape. "We got it!"

Chapter 19

At the agency, Friday's March thirtieth lunch was turned into a banquet honoring Jessica. The five interns in charge of the décor, stretched a large strip-sign on the wall that read

J E S S I C A   K E E B L E R
Thirty-two Years Of Social Service

They dressed the room with balloons and colored streamers.

Steve Gorelni flew down from Sacramento to speak glowingly of Jessica's devotion to the welfare of children and of the dramatic change in adoptions she had brought to California.

Roberta added to the high spirits of the celebration by reporting that in the week since the Liebman adoption, thirty-four applications had been received from white families asking for a mixed baby. "The extraordinary problems," she concluded, "that the large backlog of babies has caused, could soon be eased."

Cheers and applause greeted her summation.

When it was over, Jessica sat in her office, unable to believe the joy she felt at so many good things happening to her. Jonathan was back in school, and the dramatic increase in adoption applications; even *she* couldn't foretell how different life at the agency would be.

According to Steve, his words still rang in her head, *Jessica has given California an adoption revolution!* Her interns had hugged her, thanked her for her guidance and leadership. Steve had hugged her. Roberta had hugged her. And the White families asking for mixed babies were, with their applications, thanking her for creating the opportunity to have a baby in their homes.

Jessica was no longer alone against twelve men in a smelly chamber. A large majority of the eighty-four state legislators had agreed with her, praising her for the direction she'd chosen, and followed gladly. She, Jessica Keebler, had brought joy to many people's lives. Jessica recalled herself sitting before the twelve male apostles, fearful, angry at herself for being terrified by them. She suddenly slapped her desk and laughed. *That male gauntlet of a Health Services Committee finally agreed with me!*

She bounced out of her chair and paced the office. *The fight is over. I can relax. They agreed with me.* Jessica exhaled a long breath as if to memorialize the end of that phase of her work. She stood still and took another long breath. Exhaling, the image of closing the door on another difficult period of her life, the success of which had moved her up to extraordinary recognition, left her with a smile on her face.

She returned to her chair, leaned it back and closed her eyes. *What if the vote had gone the other way?* Jessica rolled her head slowly on the headrest at the disaster that that would have been. *What if the Liebmans hadn't asked?* Her eyes popped open. *What if they hadn't asked? Would it ever have occurred to me?* She smiled again, so very grateful. *Blessings on you, Liebmans.*

A knock on the door and a head poked in.

"Roberta."

"After all the excitement, Jessica, I...I didn't want to be...alone in my office. It's difficult to concentrate."

Walking toward Roberta, Jessica laughed. "No one expects you or anyone to work this afternoon." Jessica opened the door fully and hugged her. "Thank you for everything, Roberta."

"Thank *you*, Jessica."

They sat and grinned to each other for a moment, enjoying the still-actively glowing aura of the banquet. Slim, trim Roberta held herself ramrod straight as usual, her small, regular features flushed pink with pleasure. The older, fleshier Jessica slouched comfortably to reward to herself for winning the good fight, a relaxation long wished for.

"Emily has an interesting idea," Roberta said. "I wonder what you will think of it. I mentioned to her that the Liebmans are having a welcome party for their new baby tonight. She said she was very curious to see the baby in his new, White setting, if he's comfortable there."

"The baby doesn't know yet that he's a different color than others."

"No, *he* doesn't," Roberta agreed. "What Emily finally said was, she's curious to see whether or not friends of the Liebmans *really* accept the baby."

"Oh?"

"And is it…would it be ethical for the baby's social worker to make such a social visit."

Jessica was silent, thoughtful. "I don't think the line's ever been drawn that clearly. Social workers often make a final check-up visit after a case is closed," she finally said, then added, "Emily doesn't mean on an ongoing basis…"

"No, just this once, because I mentioned that apparently it's sort of an open house."

Jessica reached for the phone.

"Yes, Jessica?" Nancy asked.

"Emily, Nancy…Emily, got a minute?…Yes, here…Fine."

Emily knocked on the door and opened it.

Jessica indicated a chair. "Pull it over."

The three sat facing each other.

"Roberta said that you're interested in visiting the Liebmans," Jessica said.

Emily nodded. "Yes. From the very beginning of their application, I've…been surprised that a White family would want to raise a Negro child. I'm *still* surprised. I expressed this to Roberta at the banquet and she told me about their welcome party tonight for the baby." Emily stopped and looked at Jessica.

"And?" Jessica asked.

"Well, among Negroes it's not uncommon for us to refer to Whites as *ofays*. That's pig-Latin for *foes*. Ever since the Liebman application, I've had to say to myself, *They're not acting like ofays*. But can they really *love* a child of color? Make him part of the family?"

Jessica couldn't help smiling, having done some similar thinking about herself and Jonathan. Knowing she was teasing Emily to get to her point, she repeated, "And?"

"Would it be...ethical for a social worker to make a social call on a client...an *ex*-client?" she corrected.

Jessica's smile grew broader. "I think it would be quite professional as long as the social worker were accompanied by her director and assistant director."

To their stunned, wide-eyed looks, Jessica continued. "I've done a lot of thinking about the Liebmans, too. They *are* unusual. I'm as curious as you, Emily, about how their friends will receive Lee. Roberta, would you be up to paying the Liebman party a visit tonight?"

"Uh...you...you *do* think...it's ethical, Jessica..."

"Under these unusual circumstances, our curiosity is certainly understandable; even ethical. Looking at it positively," she continued, with a grand gesture, "Our visit could be construed as *extraordinary* professional concern."

Appreciating Jessica's banquet-high, Emily smiled.

Roberta, still cautious about transgressing standard practice, nodded. "All...right."

"I'll call to see if it's all right with them.," Jessica said. She picked up the phone and dialed. Lil answered.

"Mrs. Liebman, this is Jessica Keebler at the agency."

"Yes, Mrs. Keebler."

"Congratulations again."

"Thank you."

"I understand you're having a welcome party for the baby tonight."

"Yes, we are."

"Would it be all right if I, Miss Walker and the baby's social worker stopped in for a few minutes?"

"Uh...yes...sure. That would be very nice."

"Good. Thank you. We'll see you later. 'Bye."

"Bye."

Jessica cradled the phone and looked at the others. "We are welcome."

Tears sprang to Emily's eyes.

"What is it, Emily?"

"I...I don't know. Just the thought of seeing Lee again..."

"Maybe knowing he's in good hands will help you toward closure."

Roberta spoke up. "Let's meet at the agency at seven. That should get us there between seven-thirty and eight. I'll drive since I know the way."

"Good," said Jessica.

Emily nodded her agreement.

Jeannette and Helen arrived early and set up a long, portable massage table with tablecloth, plastic forks, spoons and paper-plates for a pot-luck smorgasbord of each person's favorite dish. They stretched a large, strip banner on the living-room wall above the table, which read,

W E L C O M E   M E E - W A H!

Friends arrived in a steady stream. The long, curving driveway to the house was quickly a solid line of cars. Later arrivals parked down on the cul-de-sac and walked up the stairs. When Roberta's car approached, there was just enough space for it without the rear bumper sticking out into Lakeshore Avenue. Waiting for Roberta to lock her car, Jessica and Emily looked above the jam of cars at the brightly-lit house on the left side of the hill.

"Picturesque," Jessica said.

Roberta gestured towards the steps in the center of the hill. "We walk, ladies."

"We get our exercise too," Emily said with a nervous smile.

The hum of voices grew louder as they approached the house. Through the large window on the patio side, they saw people sitting, standing, talking, holding drinks and plates of food. Lil answered their knock on the door. "Welcome, welcome," she said, shaking hands with each of them. The newcomers stepped onto the now enclosed porch.

"Somebody has a lot of windows to clean," Emily remarked with a half-smile.

"Yes," Lil agreed. The door to the living room on their right was open for ventilation.

"Come in. Come in."

Some people were sitting on folding chairs that George had brought from the studio.

Emily's eyes, unconsciously searching among the white faces, found the dark skins of Bessie Johnson and Tildee Larkin and her husband John. They'd come as representatives of the parent group in Watts. Emily was surprised and pleased to find them there. She had an impulse to work her way through the others and talk to them, ask them how it is, knowing the Liebmans as people. The others in the room were mostly adult students of the Liebmans, like Jeannette and Helen, or parents of child students. A few, like Tildee Larkin had brought husbands.

Amy had invited two of her friends from the Young Dancers, Cappy and Virginia.

After many introductions interrupted their eating and drinking their fill, the teenies had escaped to the privacy of Amy's new room, to sip their Styrofoam punch refills and talk teen talk.

Emily's eyes eventually found the baby sitting on George's lap. It was a shock to see him sitting up, his black eyes blown wider than usual by being among so many people. He moved his head constantly to follow their sounds and movements. She saw George stroke his back to let him know that what was happening was fine. At times George tried to cuddle the baby to soothe him, but Mee-Wah resisted, pulling himself upright again. Although he'd been with the Liebmans only eight days, Emily saw him attempt, in his mute way, to understand what was going on around him. She enjoyed seeing his active response. But he didn't smile.

She recalled the many times she held and talked to him. *No, I don't ever remember him smiling.*

While exuberance bubbled throughout the house, Jessica and

Roberta were aware that everyone was wonderfully sensitive not to overwhelm the eight-month old baby on George's lap. They heard parents laugh over recollected telling of their mother-baby experiences, but Jessica and Roberta also felt a palpable restraint to the noise level. Voices seemed to be careful not to explode and frighten.

Emily worked her way over to Bessie Johnson, a chunky lady in a dark, printed dress. Her straightened hair framed her face that shone happily. Apparently she was glad to be there, glad for the occasion. Emily offered her hand. "I'm Emily Karelin, the baby's social worker."

"Bessie Johnson, Miss Karelin." They shook hands. "The baby's social worker?"

"Yes, I supervised the care of the baby until he was adopted."

"God bless you, Miss Karelin.

Emily smiled and nodded. "Thank you."

"And God bless the Liebmans." Bessie pointed to a bridge table that had been improvised into holding gifts. Small boxed gifts were few, but there were many cards, opened and standing on end, available to be read. "We wrote that on that big card standing up. *God bless you for what you have done.*" She leaned toward Miss Karelin. "One more of our children who won't end up on the street."

Emily smiled and nodded her agreement. "Are you one of Mrs. Liebman's students?"

Bessie's head went up as she laughed heartily. "Heavens no. My eight-year-old, Odette, is in the Watts class that George teaches. And bless him for that."

Emily felt a need to hold Lee one more time. "Nice talking to you, Mrs. Johnson. I want to say hello to the baby once more…and say goodbye…and wish him luck."

"Yes, yes. We all wish him luck. Keep up your good work, Miss Karelin."

Emily smiled and nodded again. She saw George standing, holding the baby. She looked at her watch. Eight-twenty. Fearful that he might take the baby to his room to sleep, she took a step toward the baby, but a repeated clinking on a crystal glass rang out, asking everyone's attention. The noise level quickly dropped to zero.

Almost in touching distance of the baby, Emily stood still. Lil was speaking, but shorter than people around her, she was difficult to see.

"We would like to thank three people who helped us so much with the adoption. Miss Karelin, the baby's social worker, Miss Walker, the Liebmans' social worker and the director of the agency, Mrs. Keebler. Will the three of you raise your hands? Yes," she added, "they're here tonight." The three hands rose tentatively. "We would like you to applaud them quietly for all they have done."

The chatter of restrained applause bolted the baby upright again, turning his head continuously to understand the new sound.

The three acknowledged the applause with smiles and soundless thank yous.

As the applause subsided and party noises rose again, Emily moved to George. "May I hold him, Mr. Liebman?"

At the sound of her voice, Mee-Wah turned. He'd had no reason to bond with any of his three foster families. His only safe haven had been Emily's once-a-week visits, when she held and talked to him. No, he didn't smile to her now. He hadn't learned that yet, nor did he reach his arms toward her, but clearly he knew her. His inability to tell her he knew she was the nice lady who held him once a week, filled Emily's eyes with tears. "May…may I hold him, Mr. Liebman?"

"Yes. Yes, Miss Karelin." He lifted the baby to her.

In a smooth, practiced gesture she held him to her. She felt him relax and fit himself into her. "Hello, baby," she cooed, "so nice to see you again." She caressed his back. Emily knew she must not prolong it unreasonably. "You will have a good life," she whispered, "with these good people." She kissed his cheek, longer than she thought she would. "Goodbye," she whispered, "goodbye," and lifted him back to Mr. Liebman. "Thank you," she said bravely, "and good luck."

"Thank you. And thank you for coming."

Emily nodded and felt she had to move quickly or she would

break down. People were beginning to say their goodnights. Fortunately, there was no further obligation to stay. She turned quickly to find Roberta. Because the last ones in had to be the first ones out to allow others to leave, Roberta was looking for Emily and Jessica. Nodding and repeating goodnights to others as they moved, they were out the door and on the patio. Roberta guided them to the steps and down.

While Roberta unlocked the car, Emily said to Jessica, "I'll sit in the back." As the car rolled slowly around the Lakeshore curves toward Sunset Boulevard, Emily let herself cry quietly.

After everyone left, Lil took over. She suddenly felt pressured by Saturday's seven-hour teaching schedule starting at nine in the morning. "Amy, straighten up the living room a little. George and I will bathe and change the baby."

Amy grumbled to herself but went to work. She was rewarded when she went into the baby's room to hug and kiss him goodnight. He smelled baby sweet. She handed him to Lil for her hug and goodnight kiss, then Lil lifted him to George. Though still noticeably bony, the bones were soft and yielding. George held him in a hug for a moment, kissed him, then bent to lay him in his crib and draw the light blankets over him.

Lil and George sat in his room, watching him until he fell asleep, then went in to talk with Amy and say goodnight.

Printed in the United States
1371300001B/427-459

9 781592 869077